C000135438

Escaping from
the Kaiser

Escaping from the Kaiser

The Dramatic Experiences of a Tommy PoW

H. W. Tustin

Pen & Sword
MILITARY

First published in Great Britain in 2014 by
PEN & SWORD MILITARY
an imprint of
Pen & Sword Books Ltd
47 Church Street
Barnsley
South Yorkshire
S70 2AS

Copyright © Richard Corr, 2014

ISBN 978-1-47382-194-1

The right of H. W. Tustin to be identified as the author of this work has been asserted by him in accordance with the Copyright, Designs and Patents Act 1988.

A CIP catalogue record for this book is available from the British Library.

All rights reserved. No part of this book may be reproduced or transmitted in any form or by any means, electronic or mechanical including photocopying, recording or by any information storage and retrieval system, without permission from the Publisher in writing.

Typeset by Concept, Huddersfield, West Yorkshire, HD4 5JL.
Printed and bound in England by CPI Group (UK) Ltd, Croydon CR0 4YY.

Pen & Sword Books Ltd incorporates the imprints of Pen & Sword Archaeology, Atlas, Aviation, Battleground, Discovery, Family History, History, Maritime, Military, Naval, Politics, Railways, Select, Social History, Transport, True Crime, and Claymore Press, Frontline Books, Leo Cooper, Praetorian Press, Remember When, Seaforth Publishing and Wharncliffe.

For a complete list of Pen & Sword titles please contact
PEN & SWORD BOOKS LIMITED
47 Church Street, Barnsley, South Yorkshire, S70 2AS, England
E-mail: enquiries@pen-and-sword.co.uk
Website: www.pen-and-sword.co.uk

Dedication
Dedicated to my comrade, J. G. BURK,
once of the 90th Winnipeg Rifles,
by H. W. TUSTIN,
once of the 8th Durhams.

Contents

List of Plates

A crowd of some thousand newly arrived prisoners at Rennbahn camp, 1916.

The arrival of the camp commander, General Herr von Steinecke.

The general and his aide-de-camp passing the sentry guards at one of the entrances.

Outside the parcels office, New Year's Day, 1916.

Interior of Rennbahn church with the English and French pastors.

French Symphony Orchestra.

The author (standing, 5th from the left) at Rennbahn with a group of French members of the '*Caisse de Secours*'.

A scene from *Mon bébé*, an 'especially memorable' production by the French, in which all roles, male and female were enacted by men.

The *Rennbahn Church Times*, No. 4., December 1915.

Christmas card, 1915, printed at Rennbahn.

Oil painting of Rennbahn Camp (1917) by Auguste Potage, from Stadtarchiv Münster, Archivische Sammlungen, Fotosammlung Nr. 3736; reproduced by kind permission.

Prison *Lagergeld* (camp money).

A view of Block I.

A German lesson.

'Coucher', the author's sparring partner.

Photographs of Gerrie Burk.

Original map, drawn in camp, one of several maps carried by the escapees.

Tustin's 1916 British War Office map of the Münster area.

Excerpt from the author's 'escape' diary, 10–16 September.

A portion of the Dutch newspaper *De Telegraaf* found by the escapees.

Enschede, the Dutch frontier town that signalled freedom for the two escapees.

Enschede police station.

The prisoner-of-war cemetery in Münster, with its war memorial.

The author with members of his family outside the family home in Ponteland in 1917.

Reunited sweethearts Herbert and Sybil.

The author as a cadet in February 1917.

Herbert and Sybil's wedding day on 3 August 1921.

Herbert Tustin with wife Sybil, daughter Lynette and son Graham, in Teesdale, *c.*1936.

List of Illustrations

Foreword

The writing of this book gives me an opportunity long desired of expressing my gratitude to all those who sent parcels of food and clothing to us *Gefangeners* (prisoners) during the Great War. But for this kindness, the prisoners' cemeteries would have been very much larger.

While several books have been written from the point of view of the captured commissioned officer, few, if any, private soldiers have published an account of their experiences in Germany. The reason for this may be that the non-commissioned prisoner was so badly treated that he shrinks from recalling his captivity. The officer was better off. He was spared the agony of working for the enemy and the brutalities by which this slavery was enforced upon his less fortunate subordinates. He usually had better food and more leisure in which to plan and provide for escape. The aim of this book is to give as faithful an impression as possible of life in *Lager* 2 Münster i.W. during 1915 and 1916. The incidents recorded happened exactly as stated but, since the writer would dislike seeing his own name in another man's book, British names are for the most part fictitious.

Herbert Tustin
Middleton-in-Teesdale
March, 1931

Acknowledgements

I would like to thank my grandfather for writing this memoir and my grandmother, Uncle Graham and mother for preserving it and passing it down the family line. I am also indebted to my mother's Canadian cousin, Elaine Sinclair, for her important groundwork in tracing Gerrie Burk's family members, a task made all the more difficult as it was accomplished pre-internet. Thanks are also due to Richard van Emden, for reading the memoir and recommending Pen and Sword Books, and to Sue Hayter, the archivist at Burk's old college, St Andrew's (in Ontario, Canada). I would also like to thank Amélie Handke for her copy-editing help, and Julia Annandale (and her husband, Charles) for sending me the audio recording of her grandfather, Private William Stephenson. Finally, I would like to thank the many relatives of Gerrie Burk, who have been most generous in sharing information, memories and family photos.

Richard Corr
(grandson of Herbert Tustin)
London, October 2014

Introduction

This memoir of Herbert Tustin, my grandfather, only recently came into my branch of the family, having languished for several decades in an uncle's cupboard following my grandmother's demise. Unfortunately, I never met my grandfather, who died in 1939 when my mother was aged only 10. However, having grown up hearing the story of his exciting wartime adventures, I was delighted to finally get my hands on his manuscript. Reading it was quite a revelation. Not only was it dramatic and well written but also a fascinating historical document, providing a thorough and vivid description of life in a German PoW camp during the Great War. By way of a tribute to my late grandfather, I decided to see if any publishers were interested. Renowned First World War historian Richard van Emden kindly read the memoir and recommended his own publisher, Pen & Sword Books. Thankfully, they liked it, and I am very grateful to them for enabling my grandfather to share his amazing story. My now 85-year-old mother, who clearly adored her father, is delighted to see the publication of his wartime memoir; one of her proudest memories is a chance remark made by an old man during a visit to her northern hometown, Middleton-in-Teesdale, many years after her father had died: 'Ee bah Gox, tha's Tustin's lass! I'd know thee anywhere. Tha's just like thee fadder.'

My grandfather and his Canadian fellow escapee, Gerrie Burk, were both captured during the Second Battle of Ypres. This began on 22 April 1915, when the Germans launched a surprise gas attack: these attacks, the first mass use by Germany of poison gas on the Western Front, had a devastating effect, killing 6,000 men in just ten minutes and leaving a four-mile gap in the Allied lines. The reinforcements that were rushed in to plug this gap consisted primarily of Canadian and British troops, which accounted for Burk's and, a few days later, my grandfather's presence in the battle. Burk came off rather worse than my grandfather, being, in his own words, 'in pretty bad shape' from the effects of the German gas. Vast numbers of men were killed and captured, but the Allies, though pushed back, held on to the town of Ypres.

Following his capture, my grandfather spent sixteen months at Rennbahn PoW camp, situated about four miles south of Münster, on what is now Hammer Strasse, between the city and village of Hiltrup. Otherwise known as Münster II, it was built on a *Rennbahn* (race-course), with the grandstand providing space for offices, a chapel and a theatre. Rennbahn, one of nearly 300 German PoW camps, was a *Mannschaftslager*, a camp for ordinary soldiers as opposed to the *Offizierslager*, which were the camps designated for commissioned officers. The officer camps were smaller and less crowded than those for the ordinary soldiers, with better living conditions and an exemption from the requirement to do any work. They were usually established in pre-existing buildings, such as country houses, hotels and castles, whereas the ordinary soldiers were housed in huge purpose-built wooden encampments that could hold thousands of men. Rennbahn was a fairly typical *Mannschaftslager* and at times held up to 10,000 prisoners of many different nationalities.

The experience of being a PoW could be quite contrasting, depending largely on which camp the prisoner was sent to and the nature of the prison work once there. Rennbahn was, fortunately, one of the better camps, which had much to do with the decency of the officer in charge, General von Steinecke, who ruled with a gentler hand than most commandants. The other main variable in deciding a prisoner's fate was the type of assigned prison work. My grandfather was one of the luckier ones: after a brief period of being made to work for the enemy, he was offered a job within the camp as British representative on the central committee of the *Caisse de Secours* (a relief fund for necessitous prisoners), which exempted him from working parties and 'fatigues' (menial tasks).

Gerrie Burk's experience of PoW work was in stark contrast to my grandfather's, being more difficult and, for the most part, taking place outside the main camp in *Arbeitskommandos* (working parties). Rennbahn was, as my grandfather points out, merely a central area camp that supplied labour to German industry, with only 'a very small percentage [enjoying] its comparative comfort for more than a month or so before being sent away on some working party or other'. My grandfather was fortunate in that he became part of this 'very small percentage'. Burk, on the other hand, not only spent much of his time away from the camp on work detail, but also drew the short straw of being sent to the dreaded coke ovens. Here he was forced to work for a month without a day's rest, before being transferred to the mines at Castrop, where he worked for a further four months. Mining was exhausting and dangerous work, especially for malnourished men, and many PoWs suffered terribly in doing work that a British wartime report described as 'a singularly cruel and dangerous form of slavery'.[1] Indeed, Burk's military service files record that he was 'cruelly abused' while working at the coke ovens and at Castrop mines. Having survived the mines, Burk was removed to Kattenvenne, where he dug ditches and mended roads, after which he returned to Münster; here he was employed grooming horses and subsequently spent time working in the English parcels department.

The official figure for British and Empire troops captured on the Western Front during the First World War is 175,624; it is not known how many escape attempts were made, but only a small percentage were successful: altogether, there were 573 'home runs' (successful escapes).[2] Officers were more likely than other ranks to attempt an escape, having more leisure time to plan and prepare, being subject to less severe punishments should they be caught and also, given their position of command, feeling a greater obligation to return to their units.

Nevertheless, ordinary soldiers, such as my grandfather and Burk, also felt a strong urge to regain their liberty, not least on account of the harsher conditions under which they were held. Most escapes occurred from work *Kommandos*, where the prisoners were less well guarded and had more opportunities to break away. Attempting to escape from within a German PoW camp was a greater challenge, which generally required far more preparation and planning. Having escaped the camp or *Kommando*, prisoners then faced the daunting challenge of crossing enemy territory and reaching a neutral country, which was usually Holland.

Individual circumstances would have given certain prisoners a greater incentive to attempt an escape. In this context, quite remarkably – in the final proof-reading stage of this book – I was sent a recording of an interview with Private William Stephenson (1894–1995), my grandfather's friend and comrade in the 8th Durhams, where he speaks about 'Tutty' (my grandfather's nickname) and reveals a hitherto unknown reason for my grandfather's decision to escape:

Now, in the case of Tutty, ... he was very keen on a nice looking girl, also very tall. And she was called Sybil ... But, Tutty was taken prisoner of war and sent to Münster in Germany. And he had word one day – well, he told me himself – to say that there was a young lieutenant across here who's paying far more attention to Sybil than was good for Tutty's state of mind, you see, his state of health. So, Tutty and a Canadian escaped.

Stephenson knew my grandfather well, having attended the same Durham teacher-training college and having fought alongside him at Ypres, so his account is probably accurate. Considering this, my grandfather's last surviving pre-escape letter to Sybil, written on 26 July 1916, shortly before his escape, is especially poignant. The letter (the first page is shown on page 175) is uncharacteristically emotional, with my grandfather cursing his luck, speaking of his 'fevered mind' and revealing anxieties about his relationship with Sybil. Thankfully, he returned home in time to claim her as his own, and the 'young lieutenant' was, I am happy to report, never heard of again!

Once my grandfather and Burk had broken free from Rennbahn, the odds of reaching the Dutch border were not good as the majority of escaped prisoners were soon recaptured. My grandfather certainly chose well in picking a Canadian as his fellow escapee: the Canadian-British had a higher rate of successful escapes than the 'British'-British, which has been attributed to their love of the outdoors and superior ability to live off the land.[3] Burk's outdoor knowledge and survival skills were an important factor in contributing to his and my grandfather's successful escape. Their achievement also had much to do with their wise decision to avoid roads and people, which was the undoing of many other escapees. By travelling through fields and woods and keeping out of sight, their journey took longer, but was ultimately successful.

In preparing this book for publication, I have made many fascinating discoveries: in my background reading, my visits to libraries and museums and through tracing the relatives of my grandfather's fellow escapee, Gerrie Burk. This has given me a much better understanding of the experiences of my grandfather and the period in which he lived, although many questions remain. The subject of prisoners of war in Germany during the First World War is one that has been little covered by historical research. I hope, therefore, that my grandfather's memoir makes some small contribution to improving this situation. While there is always more to discover, I am grateful that my own relative's role in the Great War has been so well documented, unlike millions of his comrades, whose individual roles and adventures in the conflict will forever remain lost to history.

Post-escape biographies

Herbert Tustin described himself as a 'lucky man'. For a lucky man he certainly suffered a lot of hardship, but, considering the trials and tribulations of his wartime generation, he had perhaps good reason to consider himself fortunate: he survived the horror of Ypres; subsequent imprisonment in a German PoW camp; a perilous escape, where he was shot at by frontier guards; and the hazardous voyage back to England across the mine-strewn, submarine-infested North Sea.

His good luck held out when, following his commission in 1917 and a posting to serve in South Africa with the Royal Garrison Artillery, the SS *Kenilworth Castle* transported him safely across the seas: sailing in protective convoy to guard against the ever-present U-boat threat, he arrived in Cape Town on 27 December 1917. Away from the front line he seemed to be out of danger, but in late September 1918, the deadly 'Spanish Flu' swept through the town, killing 4 per cent of the entire population within just four weeks of its outbreak. The pandemic was unusual in that it posed the greatest risk to healthy young adults such as my grandfather, but, once again, his good luck saw him through the crisis.

My grandfather may have ridden his luck during the war, but the years that followed were marked by family tragedy: within a month of his return his mother died (aged 48); and then, a year later, his father also died (aged 50). If losing both parents at such a young age wasn't bad enough, my grandfather then suffered the tragic loss of his sister Elaine, who committed suicide in 1923.

While dealing with these losses, my grandfather worked hard to resume his career in teaching. Like others who had fought for 'a land fit for heroes', he might have expected some acknowledgement of his effort and sacrifice. However, he had to start at the bottom of the pay scale, while those with whom he had been at college, who had stayed at home rather than serve, were being paid much more. Matters came to a head when my aggrieved grandfather approached his school director to ask for a higher salary. My grandmother's diary records the stormy exchange:

'So I am to be penalised,' concluded my grandfather indignantly, 'because I volunteered to serve my country and went out with my territorial unit, though I had obtained my teacher's certificate.'

'Take that back! Take that word "penalise" back at once!' shouted the director.

'I refuse to take it back,' replied my grandfather, adding, 'You can have my resignation!' before walking out.

And so my grandfather found himself out of work and subsequently had to move to a much less salubrious area, in Wheatley Hill (a mining town near Durham), to take up a new teaching post. His fiancée and soon-to-be wife, Margaret Sybil Simpson (usually known as Sybil), was also appointed to a teaching post at the same 'tough' school, so for the next sixteen months, while living at separate addresses in the same town, they were at least working closely together.

Through all his difficulties, my grandfather was fortunate in having the love and support of Sybil, my grandmother. They had met and fallen in love at St Hild and St Bede teacher-training college in Durham, just prior to the outbreak of war. Their farewell meeting, before my grandfather was sent overseas, was a rather formal affair held in the college principal's office where, according to my grandmother, the principal and her vice-principal hovered over them like 'large benevolent female cupids'. In later years, my grandfather would say that 'it took more courage to face the ordeal of the assault of such a female stronghold than to stand firm against the enemy attack at Ypres'. During the war, my grandparents maintained their relationship through a frequent exchange of letters.

In 1921, my grandfather was appointed to a new teaching position in Middleton-in-Teesdale, where he was to remain for the rest of his life. Improved circumstances enabled him to marry and settle down with Sybil. Extraordinary as it seems now, married women were then legally barred from the teaching profession, so my grandmother's married status prevented her from pursuing the career for which she had trained (this law was not repealed until the *Butler Education Act* in 1944). My grandmother settled down to bringing up a family, with her first child, Graham, being born in 1923. Next, in 1929, came a daughter, Lynette (my mother); and finally, in 1934, another son, Godfrey (a Down Syndrome child, who lived for only six years).

Living in the centre of Middleton-in-Teesdale with a view overlooking the village green, my grandparents were well placed to involve themselves in the local community, which they clearly did, whether it be in amateur dramatics, the Literary and Debating Society, local politics (my grandfather was elected onto the local council) or the British Legion. They also enjoyed an artistic and creative life: my grandfather played the organ and piano, while my grandmother was a prolific writer and poet, often writing under the *nom de plume* 'Elad' ('Dale' spelt backwards). Once settled, my grandfather also found time to write this wartime memoir, which his wife helped edit; a fine writer herself, my grandmother may well be responsible for some of the book's more poetic turns of phrase.

Like his parents, my grandfather died young, succumbing to cancer in 1939, aged only 46. His obituary in the local newspaper attests to a 'most honourable' man who was 'held in the highest esteem wherever he lived and moved'.

Gerrie Burk, following his successful escape and just three days after reaching the apparent safety of England, had the great misfortune to be involved in a bus accident in London. This accident, added to his ordeals in Germany, severely affected his already strained nerves, and on returning to Canada in November 1916, it was recommended that he go to a military convalescent hospital in Victoria, British Columbia. Happily, following a period of rehabilitation, Burk recovered to lead a full and productive life, despite (according to his niece, Connie Sepulchre) suffering all his life from the gassing in Flanders. Following his escape, he played no further part in the war and was discharged from the army in July 1918.

In 1923, Burk married Caroline 'Smokey' Smallacombe, with whom he was to have two children. He went on to have a long and successful career, from 1923 to 1955, as the agent in charge of Indian affairs for Northern Ontario. Burk's unremitting efforts to improve the conditions of the Indian people under his charge show that he was as much a hero in civilian life as he was during the war: the evidence supporting this is laid out in an academic paper by Mark Kuhlberg:

> He [Burk] chose to ignore the department's prevailing racist ideology in favour of nurturing the incipient desire for industry and enterprise that he saw first-hand among the Aboriginal constituents of his agency. In the process, he was compelled to overcome numerous obstacles that Indian Affairs placed in his way. As a result, Burk's career stands as a glowing testament to the

indomitable spirit of one departmental official's commitment to assisting the Aboriginal peoples.[4]

In her memoir, Connie Sepulchre describes her Uncle Gerrie as a jolly and 'effervescent' man who was 'almost always laughing or joking'. Although afflicted with a speech impediment (my grandfather does not mention Burk's stammer, a disclosure that he would have presumably regarded as ungentlemanly), he was a great teller of humorous shaggy dog stories. However, like so many of his Great War comrades, he did not care to talk about his wartime experiences and, unlike my grandfather, left no written memoir. I have only been able to find out what I have through consulting his family, newspaper clippings and military records. Of Burk's pre-escape wartime adventures, little is known: the story behind the scar over his right eye, which his military service papers record as the result of a blow from a German while a prisoner, was possibly too painful to recall, and one can only imagine what other dramatic tales he kept locked away. Indeed, his grandson, Burk Quintrell, remarks that the subject of the war and his escape was best avoided as even in later years, it would bring tears to his eyes. His family can now, at least, read my grandfather's memoir to help fill in the story of his amazing and dramatic escape, while I have been privileged to find out more about the man without whom my grandfather might not have survived to write this memoir, let alone marry and start a family. I am delighted to discover that Gerrie Burk lived a long, adventurous and productive life and grew old surrounded by his family, who loved and cared for him. He died in 1974, aged 85.

Richard Corr (grandson of Herbert Tustin)
London, October 2014

1. Government Committee on the Treatment by the Enemy of British Prisoners of War, *Report on the Employment in Coal and Salt Mines of the British Prisoners of War in Germany* (HMSO, London, 1918), p. 2.
2. *Statistics of the Military Effort of the British Empire during the Great War, 1914–1920* (HMSO, London, 1922), p. 329.
3. This point is made in an excellent and recently published book by John Lewis-Stempel, *The War Behind the Wire: The Life, Death and Glory of British Prisoners of War, 1914–18* (Weidenfeld and Nicolson, London, 2014), p. 220.
4. Mark Kuhlberg, '"Mr. Burk is most interested in their welfare": J.G. Burk's campaign to help the Anishinabeg of Northwestern Ontario, 1923–53', *Journal of Canadian Studies/Revue d'études canadiennes*, Vol. 45, No. 1 (Winter 2011), pp. 58–89.

Chapter 1

A Glimpse of the Battle of Ypres, April 1915

A hen fluttering down from its perch on to my face aroused me. I struck at it angrily and it flew squawking through the window amid the guffaws of my companions, leaving a scurry of feathers behind it. The stench of a sodden pigsty steamed up through the loose boards of the hen loft which formed our billet, overpowering the sour smell of the soiled hay which made our common bed.

It was not a sweet billet this; but neither the hens above nor the pigs below had disturbed us, nor the miasmal vapour that drifted in through a shattered window from the great manure heap in the farm-yard outside. We had passed the night oblivious of the fitful glare and rumble of distant gunfire – careless even of the tearing reverberation of bombs dropped near us during this, our second night in France – for we were dog-tired, and, being Tommies of a Northern Territorial regiment, had learned to make the most of the little rest allowed.

We were still drowsy on that cold Wednesday morning of 21 April 1915, loath to leave the soft hollows that had been moulded and warmed by our tired bodies, but as a whole cascade of fowls followed the example of the pioneer which had awakened me, we stirred our-selves into activity. One or two hardy warriors bathed in the duck pond near at hand and emerged from the opaque liquid in high spirits, declaring themselves much refreshed; but the sight of their miry bodies was no encouragement for others to follow their example.

The morning was occupied in routine work and wearisome inspec-tions and parades, and then in the afternoon, we were free to explore the village of Sainte-Marie-Cappel, which lay within half a mile of our farm.

The peace of this hamlet fell upon us like a benediction. I have often wished to visit it again, to see its women gossiping on their doorsteps, its black-robed priest passing quietly among his flock, its grubby children playing on its dusty road. The war seemed far, far away. Yet as the children played there came, rising and falling on the breeze, the sinister jarring and rumbling of the guns.

Rations seemed scarce, but we found an *estaminet* (a café where beer and wine may be bought) where food and drink were good and cheap, and served to us by a demure and dark-eyed damsel. A number of us gathered there on Thursday evening and asked Suzanne for '*cochon mort avec des pommes des poulets*' (literally translated: dead pig with apples of chickens). Poor lassie!

She '*no compris*' and lifted her hands, her face expressing dismay in every feature. Our French expert repeated his order. There followed a moment's silence and then, as someone clucked like a triumphant hen and others grunted, comprehension dawned with a ripple of merry laughter.

We got on famously after that, and soon a stream of Anglo-French silliness made the colour play among Suzanne's dimples as she bustled to and fro supplying our needs – '*Mamselle promendey avec moy*'. '*Suzanne a un baiser pour Tommy?*'

'*Donney un peu d'amour.*' – But a harsh maternal voice soon interfered with the flow of nonsense by calling Suzanne behind the scenes, and we were left to console ourselves with the 'dead pig and chickens' apples'. It was a glorious feed. I could not have enjoyed it more even had I known that it was to be the last good meal I was to have for nearly eighteen months. It was indeed the last that one or two present were ever to enjoy; for next morning we marched away, and the road we took was the road towards Ypres and beyond.

The Brigade assembled at Steenvoorde on that Friday, 23 April. Here for the first time we felt close to the war. Empty motor buses moved in a ceaseless stream round the huge square on which we were paraded. Each bus stopped a few moments, filled up with troops, and then drove furiously away. As we waited I remember how keyed up we all were with intense excitement, with what keen interest we watched an air duel that was being fought out away to the east. We were full of the spirit of glorious adventure, glad at the prospect of being rushed into the heart of a great battle.

As our buses took us on through Poperinghe, our interest and excitement grew even more intense. Shell holes gaped in the fields about us; here and there a shattered house fired our indignation and made us long to get at the enemy. Occasional refugees, grey-haired men and anxious-faced women with their children limping beside them were to be seen making their way eastwards, pushing barrows or perambulators piled high with their pitiful treasures; and as each pathetic group passed us, our hate of Germany increased. We were too young and too much under the sway of the spirit of the time to see further than the immediate cause of these tragedies. We forgot all the good we knew of the Germans and thought of them collectively as the 'blond beast', gloating over the prospect of killing some of them very soon. It never occurred to us that there were young Germans feeling just the same about ourselves, and just as full of righteous indignation. We knew nothing of the German viewpoint, and our ignorance made it easy for us to hate.

On reaching Vlamertinghe, we left our buses and expected to march straight into the battle line. This seemed to us 'just round the corner', for bursts of rifle and machine gun fire came clearly to our ears. We were ordered into billets, however, for the night, and my platoon was soon ensconced in a disused cow byre, which was already occupied by a considerable number of men just settling themselves to slumber. I tried to make myself snug in the gutter which ran between the two doors, but I found that despite a windscreen I made of my equipment, a strong breeze played on my neck, tickling the whole length of my spine. It was of no use my looking for a 'better 'ole', for the gutter was the only available space remaining, the cosy stalls being crowded with more fortunate early arrivals; so I hunted round for blankets. Another late-comer was at the same game and, joining forces, it was not long before we found a pile from which we did not hesitate to borrow a couple each. After that we made the gutter a veritable snuggery.

I fell immediately into that blissful state of absolute contentment that precedes a glorious sleep. And then a lantern shone in the gloom, and a voice called for three men for guard duty. It was the voice of my platoon commander. I groaned in spirit, closing my eyes, snoring softly and feigning sleep, and prayed that the threat of night duty might pass over me. Vain prayer! The lantern shone on my face. An NCO shook me by the shoulder, and out I had to go with two other unfortunates to guard the slumber of some wretched colonel and his staff.

Our guard room was the draughty stone-flagged passage of the house that these gentlemen were using as headquarters, and when the two men off duty lay down in it alongside the lance corporal in charge of the guard, the passage was full. I was soon asleep in my blankets despite the cold stones and the wind under the doors, the noise of battle that shook the house and the din in the street – despite even the occasional discharge of a 6-inch battery not far away. It was a boot that awakened me, a heavy boot, vigorously planted in the middle of my abdomen with the weight of a heavy man behind it; an officer, returning from his rounds, trying to jump over the guard without disturbing it, had miscalculated the jump. His grunts of apology mingled with my grunts of anguish, and then I turned over to attempt sleep again.

There was no more sleep for me that night; the noise of traffic in the street had increased; the stone floor seemed to have grown colder and harder; an occasional officer came or went, stepping perforce over our bodies and eliciting tired groans and murmurings. I was half glad when my turn for sentry duty came, and I turned out to stump up and down on a beat which lay just opposite a big hospital.

Along the road before me, motor ambulances rushed almost incessantly westwards. Some of these halted at the hospital gates, to be pounced upon immediately by waiting orderlies. I was near enough to admire the deft skill and infinite care with which the RAMC men worked, as the poor broken bodies were lifted out and examined before being carried inside the gates. I stood marvelling at the tenderness they managed to combine with their speed; and then, as I watched, there came a rough, almost brutal movement, as a corpse was tossed with a thud to the ground.

I suddenly realised that in those ambulances rushing westwards men were dying, that men were dying too in that peaceful-looking building opposite, and that away beyond the trees over the fields, where flares, rising and falling, marked the front line, men were killing and being killed. As I stood listening to the bursts of musketry borne ever and anon to my ears on the night wind, and as dull explosions jarred the ground under my feet, I felt suddenly overwhelmed by a sense of the loneliness of Life and the nearness of Death. War took on a new significance. The sight and sound of one corpse flung callously to the ground affected me more than all the casualty lists I had ever scanned.

The night paled into the grey of dawn. Two nuns approached me, speaking rapid French and wringing their hands with imploring gestures. With difficulty I gathered that they wanted to go eastwards into all the hell of this great battle to help the wounded and to console the dying. Could they be allowed to travel in one of the empty ambulances returning to the Line? I referred them to an officer and watched with sympathy as he sadly shook his head and they turned miserably away.

Early on Saturday morning, our guard being dismissed, I found myself at liberty to wander round Vlamertinghe and collect news. I found one or two Canadians who told me that the enemy was launching a big attack with Ypres and the coast as its objectives; that German gas was wiping out whole regiments; that our line was broken in places and the Germans advancing. Things looked very black in Vlamertinghe on that morning of 24 April 1915.

Men of various regiments came drifting back from the Ypres direction in twos and threes. Their clothing was daubed with clay and discoloured, their faces livid, and they stumbled westwards with a tired yet hurried gait as if impelled by some horror which would not let them rest a moment. They went by without a word, ashamed to confess themselves defeated and broken in body and soul; and the sight of them was not reassuring.

I heard a story of a motor car badly damaged by a shell, which had driven into the village a few hours previously, so I went to look at it in the grounds behind the hospital. It was, or had been, a five-seater; its bonnet was shattered, its coachwork splintered, its upholstery torn and clotted with blood; blood had dripped on to the running board, and from that onto the ground below. The driver, hideously wounded, had managed to bring it to the hospital gates before he died. Beside him sat the body of a young subaltern, head and chest gaping, behind them the remains of a field officer with arms folded across a headless trunk. The wrecked car before me bore grisly testimony to the truth of the story.

Turning away, sickened by the sight and smell of blood, I stepped over some tarpaulins and sheets lying in rows upon the ground. There must have been a score or more of them. Idly curious, I stepped down and lifted a corner – to recoil in horror before the stark immobility of a corpse. The knowledge burst upon me with the shock of a blow, that under each of these covers lay the body of a man who had died in hospital or ambulance. The roots of my hair tingled. I stood alone, the only living man on this parade of Death. And I thought of the line of similar base hospitals each with its rows of dead, the line that stretched from the Dover Straits to the Alpine foothills.

We spent the day lounging about, expecting at any minute to be assembled and marched to the Line, but it was not until about 7 o'clock that Saturday evening that we left Vlamertinghe. We did not know our destination, but an ominous conversation was overheard by one of our signallers, between our colonel, a kindly civilian only half militarised, and his adjutant who was 'every inch a soldier'.

'I can't take my men up there, Adjutant! It's murder.'

'Orders are orders, Colonel,' replied the adjutant gruffly. 'We must obey them.'

For the first portion of that three- or four-hour march to Ypres, my company sung lustily. 'On Ilkley Moor' went well; so did 'Tipperary'; and an irreverent saga concerning Dives and Lazarus, with innumerable verses and a grand chorus. 'Hi-Ho-Jerum; Hi-Ho-Jerum; Glory Hallelujah! With a Hi-Ho-Jerum'.

But the tune that best suited our humour was the quadruple chant from the Cathedral Psalter: we sang it in harmony, with all manner of variations and vocal obligatos as was our Company's custom, singing without words on the broad vowel 'aw'. Despite drizzling rain, which tried to depress our spirits, we were determined to keep cheerful.

After a while, however, the enemy artillery turned our minds from music to matters less harmonious. Big shells began to riot overhead with the noise of express trains, and we were concerned to notice that they all travelled the same way. What were our own gunners doing, we wondered. One shell burst in the roadway between the tail of our column and our baggage mules, with a concussion that brought some of our younger lads flat on their faces with fright. There was no singing after that.

Ypres was a hell. Darkness had fallen, and as we doubled through the main-street, stumbling over piles of fallen masonry, the crashes of exploding shells and the rumble of collapsing stonework were far from reassuring. I remember racing by the bodies of horses and of men, and in the glare of a burning house, I noticed a woman lying dead in the roadway.

To the east of the city we rested a little while. Lines of Verey lights rising and falling on either side showed that we were well within the famous Salient. Shells continued to screech over us, to explode among the masses of rubble that had once been Ypres.

Suddenly there came shouts and the noise of galloping horses. We pressed close to the side of the road, and a battery of our field artillery dashed madly past us towards the rear. As we formed ranks again to march on through the mire and the rain, we felt that artillery in retreat was cold comfort to advancing infantry.

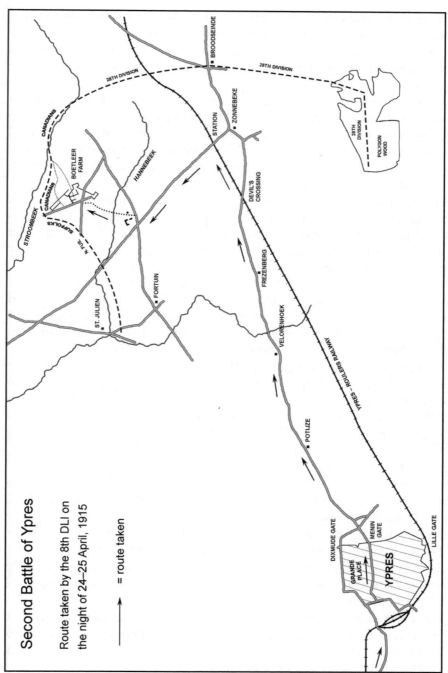

The route of the 8th Durham Light Infantry (DLI) through Ypres to the Second Battle of Ypres.

A grizzled veteran of the South African war confided his impressions. 'This is a b****!' he said hoarsely. 'There was never as many shells fired in all the b***** S. African war.' He was destined to see still more shell fire before he was himself killed by a shell some twelve hours later.

At about midnight we marched into some fields and took up a position behind a hedge: some of us began to use our trenching tools to dig ourselves in, while some lay down to sleep. The rain had increased to a heavy downpour, but I should have been glad myself to have had the chance of sleep. No chance was given, for within half an hour we were moved on.

We had another short rest at a crossroads somewhere near St Julien [Sint-Juliaan], I think. It was a foolish place for a halt; rifle bullets buzzed past or ricocheted whining from the pavé into the night. After this we left the road again and squelched through spongy mud for some time, until the approaching dawn made visible the hideous effects of the German gas. Bodies were lying about in all attitudes, their faces yellow and ghastly, mucus flowing from their mouths and nostrils. I remember our CO giving the order, 'Eyes left', as we passed to the left of a sight especially distressing to men who had never seen fighting before. Many of us, however, were hypnotised by the horror, of which we had just caught a glimpse, and were unable to turn our eyes from it. It was a huge shell-hole half full of stinking water, and in it and about it, mixed up in hideous confusion, were the remains of perhaps a dozen Scots Canadians – a tangle of heads, legs, arms, and kilts protruding from the slimy mud. A low murmur passed along our ranks, and then came our captain's voice, 'Steady lads! Eyes front!', calm and reassuring.

Ten minutes later, in the cold twilight of a wet Sunday morning, we entered our allotted trenches, marched down to them in fours and, so far as I know, we lost not a man in doing so. In fact we had lost only one man during the whole march from Vlamertinghe.

There we were, six days after leaving England, tired, hungry, sodden with rain, caked with mud, in what was at the time probably the most critical position in the whole British line, the extreme head of the Ypres Salient.

We were very inexperienced and I saw one youngster, who had climbed on the parados to have a look round, pulled down roughly by a Canadian, – 'J**** C*****! Son!' he exclaimed. 'Don't be a gor darned fool! The Hun line is under 200 yards away!'

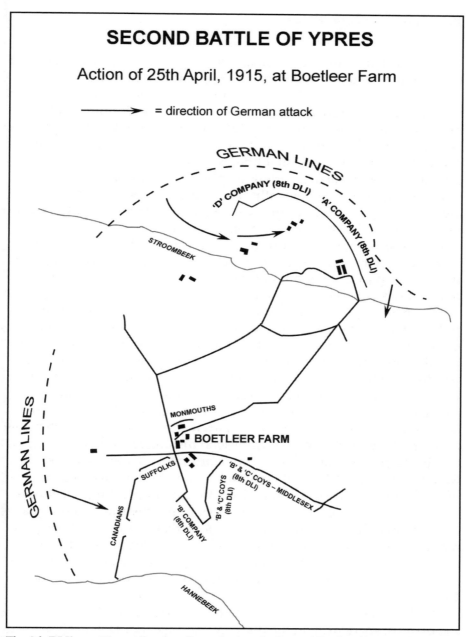

SECOND BATTLE OF YPRES

Action of 25th April, 1915, at Boetleer Farm

———→ = direction of German attack

GERMAN LINES

'D' COMPANY (8th DLI)

'A' COMPANY (8th DLI)

STROOMBEEK

GERMAN LINES

MONMOUTHS

BOETLEER FARM

SUFFOLKS

'B' & 'C' COYS – MIDDLESEX

'B' & 'C' COYS (8th DLI)

'B' COMPANY (8th DLI)

CANADIANS

HANNEBEEK

The 8th DLI's position at Boetleer Farm during the Second Battle of Ypres. The author was captured during the retirement of A Company, in which he was attached, on the night of 25 April 1915. Surrounded on three sides, the decision was made to withdraw through the remaining gap: 'The force retired under a perfect hell of fire; shells, high explosive and shrapnel, machine guns and rifles dealing out death on all sides ... The slaughter was fearful – the scene indescribable.' (*The Bede*, June 1915: *The Bede* was the magazine of the author's teacher-training college in Durham)

Another lad, without a Canadian to pull him down, was shot through the head and killed instantly about five minutes later.

There was ample evidence all about us of the severity of recent bombardment. A recess near me was smeared with human jelly, the brains or lungs of some poor boy who had been living and laughing a few hours beforehand. Gouts of blood and torn displaced sandbags showed too clearly what might be expected.

Sentries were posted at various loopholes. The Canadian companies, which we had relieved, silently filed out of the position and melted away, leaving a machine gun of theirs with their gallant crew to instruct us on the mysteries of trench warfare.

There seemed nothing for us to do but watch and wait. Through our loopholes, all that we could see was barbed wire and grass. Some of us tried to sleep in the wet mud of the fire step; one or two even tried to relieve the suspense by polishing their buttons.

The enemy's guns had almost ceased firing, but with the coming of full daylight they began again, directing fire upon the support trenches a mile or so to our rear and upon the scattered farms between these trenches and our own position. We waited anxiously for our own artillery to reply to the persistent challenge of the German guns, and after what seemed endless hours, a few shells burst close behind us. We thought they came from the rear and our spirits rose. These were surely from British guns that were firing short! It was a case of the wish being father to the thought, and we were soon disillusioned, for they turned out to be the precursors of a bombardment of our own trenches. Ringed about with fire, all communications broken, we began to be overwhelmed by a sense of utter isolation and impending catastrophe.

The shelling eased off towards noon, and then an enemy plane came skimming along our lines, so low that we could distinguish the features of its occupant. We tried in vain to bring him down with rifle and machine gun bullets, only making him rise a little higher as he returned and again indicated to his batteries the exact position of our trenches.

'We'll get hell alright now,' muttered a Canadian machine gunner as the plane droned away in the distance. And we did. Hell itself seemed to open almost immediately.

Fortunately for my platoon, the heavier guns were ranging a few yards beyond our section of trench; but to our left we could see shell upon shell bursting on the parapet and behind it and knew that men there were – as a survivor described it to me afterwards – being literally 'blown to bloody bits' among the clouds of debris which spouted continually.

For hours the fury raged unabated, missiles of all shapes and sizes ripping, whining, and squealing about us. Our senses swam in a sea of vibration as high explosives rocked our universe and swathed us in yellow fumes. Shrapnel filled the air with curiously vicious twangs and hums. Tiny fragments of grit flew continuously in all directions, tearing our clothing, ripping the skin on our hands and faces as we cringed and cowered under the hot blasts.

The man on my right dropped writhing into the trench bottom. 'I'm done for,' he groaned as I bent over him. 'It's my back.' Gingerly I put my hand under his equipment, expecting to find a sticky mess, but I felt no blood and could find no wound. As I was cutting off his pack, I suddenly noticed that it was torn and that resting loosely in the rent was the heavy base of a small shell. All that he was suffering from was bruises and shock.

Towards 5 o'clock the bombardment ceased, and German infantry could be seen in the rear. They were advancing through a gap on our left flank where troops had been annihilated in the gas attack of the previous day. Some of our best men were killed in a vain attempt to prevent the advance by using our machine guns. The gap was too wide: there must have been a mile of open ground and undefended trenches. I believe our right flank also was 'in the air'.

Some confusion ensued, due to our lack of experience and to the stupefying effects of the bombardment. We felt dazed and bewildered rather than afraid. Except for a nibble at our iron rations, we had eaten nothing for twenty-four hours; some of us had had no sleep for twice that length of time. We did not know the direction from which the main attack would come, and we fixed bayonets and waited for orders while we watched the clay in the back of our parapet stirring from time to time under the impact of bullets from the rear.

Suddenly we saw masses and lines of field grey moving towards us about a thousand yards to our rear, and some of us began to pump lead at them from a hedge behind the trenches. Our captain was standing near a machine gun, which had been placed in position behind the hedge and which seemed to be impeding the enemy considerably. We gathered confidence on seeing the calm precision with which he was using a borrowed rifle, and we enjoyed the change of shooting at something after so many hours of torturing inactivity.

The machine gun jammed occasionally. Do what we might, the grey figures of the enemy were getting near enough to afford individual targets. Their shooting was not without effect and I knew that some of our men went down. All that I can remember feeling at this time, however, was a great desire to get off as many rounds as possible. Then a man standing behind me as I knelt used my left shoulder as a rest for his rifle muzzle. I thought his discharge had taken off my head. The shock made me fall into a shell-hole from which I emerged with my rifle unusable: by bad luck, I had just been reloading as I fell, and the open breach had become so choked with mud that I could not move the bolt either forwards or backwards. This must have made me crazy for a time, for I remember pulling and tugging at that bolt in a paroxysm of impotent fury, scarring my hands on the hot barrel, blind to everything but my desire to repair the damage. I have a hazy recollection of lying on my back and trying to force out the bolt with my foot, and then I suddenly realised that our firing had ceased. Looking round, I found to my dismay that my comrades had retired and that I was alone with the advancing enemy less than fifty yards away.

I sprang to my feet in a panic, and still clutching my useless rifle, I raced blindly along the shell-scarred ground behind our front line. I saw that I was overtaking two of our men running in the same direction and felt glad at the prospect of their company, but as I neared them they both went down. Whether they were killed or wounded, I never knew, for I dared not wait to help them. I felt as if the whole German army was concentrating fire upon me, and I ran wildly on until I found a Canadian lieutenant in a kind of sand-bagged shelter. He had about half a dozen men with him and we discussed the situation. It seemed a hopeless one; the position was lost, our retreat was cut off; we had to choose between a glorious death and surrender.

We did not know what to do.

I stepped from the door of the shelter with my bayonet lowered, and then I saw a rifle muzzle not ten yards distant, a ring of steel with a hard grey eye above it. As the ring steadied, I saved my life by flinging myself to the ground. Before I could rise I was seized by rough hands, disarmed, and dragged to my feet, to find myself surrounded by sinister looking men in the hated field grey. I realised that my life was mine no longer, that I was a prisoner of war.

Chapter 2

Ypres to Rennbahn

We were made prisoners at about 7.00pm on Sunday, 25 April 1915. A few minutes previously we had been trying to kill the men who now had us in their power. What hope could we have that they would forego their revenge? Yet our lives were spared, and we were subjected to no worse brutality than a playful prod with a bayonet. We were jeered at by our triumphant captors and menaced with fists, rifle butts, and pistols, but, so far as I know, none of our little group suffered serious damage.

There were cases in other parts of the line where no quarter was given. We heard later that some of our wounded were dispatched without mercy, even our own battalion's medical officer and his orderly being shot at close quarters as they were bandaging the wounded. Ample proof is available of these atrocities in the scars that these two men carry on their heads to this day. I have seen both of them since the war and heard their story.

Actually, the Germans during the war were told as many lies about us as we were about them. They were persuaded that every English field dressing station was a nest of machine guns and that our medical men were devils who slit the throats of any German wounded that fell into their hands. Moreover, temperamentally the German is much more excitable than the Englishman, once his traditional phlegm is overcome. Indeed, my own opinion is that the legend of German stolidity is based on observation of appearance alone. At any rate, infantry soldiers of any nationality cannot be expected to exude the milk of human kindness while clearing up territory they have captured at great cost of life, in which every corner may contain all manner of lurking dangers. Atrocious deeds have been committed by soldiers of every nation, and in the suspense and stress of the moment, I felt that our lives were hanging on a very slender thread, for our captors were in a state of wild excitement, cursing and shouting, pulling and pushing, as they wrenched open our ammunition pouches and examined the clips of cartridges we had remaining. I resented their insults bitterly, unable at the time to make any allowances. I felt that they were Huns manifesting

Hunnishness; but though I longed to resist, I realised that any other attitude other than sheep-like passivity would be fatal.

After a lot of pushing and hustling, I was led away in company with another Englishman to a secluded hollow, where we were threatened with summary execution. The torrents of abuse poured forth were largely wasted upon us, for apart from odd words like '*Schweine Engländer*' and '*Dum-Dum*' we understood none of it, but we gathered that some Germans had suffered wounds which seemed due to notched or filed bullets and that we two were to pay the penalty.

I cannot remember any moment in which I felt so utterly lonely and so absolutely helpless, nor any moment when life seemed so poignantly sweet and desirable as it did on that calm Sunday evening. I watched a plane skimming peacefully in the western sky, a black silhouette against the colour of a noble sunset. Somewhere a bird was singing.

It was springtime and I longed to live.

There was no doubt, however, in my mind as to the intentions of the men around us, for they showed in pantomime exactly what was to happen. As we watched their threatening gestures, the sound of a few scattered shots suggested that other executions were taking place not far away.

'Why in hell don't they get on with it?' groaned my companion, who was in severe pain from a bullet hole in the shoulder.

There seemed to be some dispute among them. Were they waiting for some sergeant's arrival so that the correct formalities might be observed? Could it be that some were hesitant as to the legality or morality of the little affair? I wondered whether the discussion centred round the question as to whether or not to blindfold us, for one of the disputants was holding an ominous handkerchief: the orthodox German thinks curiously at times. Whatever might be the cause of the delay, it saved our lives; for suddenly a mounted officer galloped up, scattering our prospective executioners with a great display of Germanic fury, waving his sword over their heads as they fled in terror. He looked us up and down contemptuously as though we were dogs, but, moved by the sight of my companion's hanging shoulder and blood-stained tunic, tore out his own field dressing and threw it to me, signing that I was to bandage the wound. Then, after shouting orders to two men to look after us, he galloped away into the darkening shadows, leaving two Englishmen hastily revising their opinion of his race.

We were taken back to our original party and led through the German lines. Their dead lay where they had fallen, and we had to tread carefully in the gathering twilight to avoid them, while some of the German soldiers in their vicinity spat upon us, and the murmur of hate in which we moved swelled and rose to a very high key.

One or two shrapnel shells burst over our heads. We presumed that they came from some English battery, and I remember being amused at the excitement of our escort and its manifest desire to get out of danger as quickly as possible.

I had passed the stage of caring much about an odd shrapnel shell or two, and I was too weary to run until stimulated by a dig in the ribs from the business end of a large automatic held in the shaking hand of a stout German NCO, who looked half-crazy with fear and excitement. '*Vek*! ('*weg*' = away, i.e. Go away! Get lost!) *Los*! *Schweine!*' he yelled in a cracked falsetto. '*Schneller. Schneller gehen*!', or something like that. So I had to '*Vek*' until we were out of danger.

Our little party was like the proverbial snowball. By the time we reached a road, our number must have increased to almost a hundred, by driblets of men captured in different parts of the district. Each little group had imagined that its members were the only soldiers captured. We all felt that if only we could have got together an hour or so earlier, we could have fought our way back to Ypres.

How weary and dejected we were as we trudged mechanically along that road, cold and hungry! I thought even then of escape but dismissed the idea as entirely out of the question for the time being: it was a dark night without stars, and I had lost all sense of direction: we were very strongly escorted, guards on each side, one to every four men: and anyway I was too desperately tired to do anything but march, of no use to myself or to anyone else.

There were short rests about every hour, rests which enabled some of us to drop in our tracks upon the road and sleep. I seemed to sleep as I marched. The memory of that night is as the memory of a dream.

At about midnight the dragging limp of our wretched column shuffled to a halt outside a large church in a small town, the name of which I have never known [Roulers; Flemish name = Roeselare]; and after some delay during which I slept on the pavement, we were herded into this building. I cannot remember lying down, but I do remember being stirred to consciousness by the boot of a German officer, who ordered me to get up from the floor and signed to me to make a bed of chairs. I suppose that he meant to be kindly and that he imagined a stone floor was harmful to me, but I would have thanked him for leaving me alone, and I obeyed his orders grudgingly enough. I shared my new bed with another prisoner. Without blankets and food, we felt the cold intensely now that we had been roused from sleep, so we unbound our puttees and used them to tie ourselves tightly together, making one large wrapping of our combined great-coats, so that each might benefit from the other's warmth, and I knew no more until 6.00am on Monday morning when 'coffee' and 'bread' were issued.

This coffee was a curious beverage, made, I believe, of burnt grain and acorns flavoured with chicory, but it was wet and warm and com-forting: with milk and sugar it would have been agreeable; in fact, I learned to like it before I returned home. The bread was beastly, a dark brown dough that seemed compounded of rotten potatoes and saw-dust; but we ate it and longed for more.

It was strange, as we ate this meagre breakfast, to see the morning light dimly filtering through stained-glass windows upon fluted pillars and images of saints, and to hear, echoing along the aisles of this beautiful Gothic building, the raucous voices of our guards.

Within a couple of hours after I awakened, we were taken in street cars to the Belgian town of Courtrai and lodged in the civil prison there, ten or twelve of us in a cell.

But for the ever-gnawing consciousness that we were merely dere-licts, jetsam of battle, beaten and useless, and but for the weak lassi-tude caused by hunger, we should have found this gaol a pleasant billet. With plenty of good clean straw for bedding, we were warm and dry, allowed to visit friends in other cells and to watch the civil prisoners working about the place; we were humanely treated in every way, in fact the sole complaint I had about Courtrai gaol was its dietary.

The food seemed insufficient to keep us alive, but before leaving German control I revised my estimate of the amount of nourishment necessary to maintain life.

We killed time dozing in our luxurious straw, chatting about the military situation and comparing experiences, while we tried as best we could to delouse ourselves. Some of us found bullet holes in our clothing, which we had not previously noticed; I found three, one of them drilled neatly through my cap. There was the inevitable bullet-plugged Bible, but Jackson, its owner, was a notorious joker and was suspected of having shot at it himself in order to be able to show a

sensational relic. 'Made in England,' we teased him. Harrison's cigarette case was much more remarkable than Jackson's Bible, having
undoubtedly saved its owner's life by deflecting a bullet away from his
heart round the curve of his ribs. He proudly displayed the damaged
metal case and showed us a cut in his shirt, declaring that even though
his very singlet was slit for half an inch, his skin was not scratched.

Our yarning was disturbed from time to time as we were taken, each
in turn, for examination by a German Intelligence Officer, a decent
fellow, amazingly well informed. He knew all about us, where we had
trained and when we left England, and he spoke perfect English.

'What chance do you think you have of beating us?' was one of the
questions put to me that I felt I could answer quite frankly, and he did
not like my reply.

'It is not a question of chance at all, sir, but merely one of time,' I said
cheerfully. He dismissed me with a scowl and a grunt, and I returned
light-heartedly to my comrades, whom I found exchanging views with
a German corporal and expressing their opinion that Deutschland was
'kapoot'.

'Kapoot' (Ger. *kaputt*, broken) was one of the first German words I
learned. My braces had broken and I tried in vain to obtain string for
the necessary repairs, with one hand holding up my sagging nether
garments and with the other dangling the forlorn remains of my braces
before the eyes of every guard whom I judged to have a trace of
benevolence in his physiognomy. All that I received, however, by way
of help, was a succession of grunts, sometimes sympathetic, sometimes hostile, and the word 'kapoot' repeated many times, so that I
understood that it might be correctly applied to anything that was
completely broken and useless. I had to knot the two portions of braces
together and use them as a belt for many an uncomfortable month.

Our stay at Courtrai ended on Wednesday, 28 April. There was
great excitement among the military as we were marched through the
town from the gaol to the railway station amid the usual abusive yells,
brandished swords, and menacing pistols. The escort was perhaps
anxious to impress the sympathetic Belgian population which lined
the pavements, watching with sad eyes this march of the English
towards Germany. One woman broke through the cordon of guards to
give some little pack, perhaps chocolate, to a prisoner a few yards in
front of me; she succeeded in her intention, and then I saw her
stretched full length on the roadside by a ruthless blow on the breast
with the butt of a rifle.

The haste and excitement and ill temper with which we were hustled into cattle trucks at the station made us hope that an allied advance was already threatening Courtrai; and as we rattled and bumped through Machlin [Machelen?] and Deuze [Deinze?] to Gent, we kept that hope alive for all we were worth, imagining a great and glorious break through Belgium, which would culminate in a complete German surrender. But, in our hearts, we knew we were talking 'hot air'.

What a journey this was! But for the fact that I kept a brief diary, I should find it hard now to believe that it occupied only three days, for memory records it as an interminable period of misery and hunger. Our great desire was for food. We even grubbed about on the dirty floor in search of anything edible, one man being lucky enough to discover a leek trampled among the filth and generous enough to offer me half of it: I remember the shameful greed with which we ate this small luxury and how we groped about in the semi-darkness searching in vain for more.

Once we had a great treat. Our trucks were shunted into a siding; we were ordered to get out; and then we were taken into some railway sheds where we sat on benches at rows of trestle tables and were each given a bowl of good thick soup, steaming hot. For the rest of the journey, the daily bread ration – a hunch of sour dough measuring about 4" by 2" and 1½" thick – had to suffice, washed down with a dish of 'coffee'.

We passed through Lüttich [Fr. Liège] and Stellwerk [*Stellwerk* is German for 'signal box', so a sign showing this was probably misinterpreted as being a station named Stellwerk], and on Friday a glimpse of a board bearing the words 'Auchen Hof' ['Aachen Hbf'? Hbf = Ger. *Hauptbahnhof* (Engl. mainline station)] told me we were in Germany. There were other signs that we had crossed the frontier, for it was now dangerous when in stations to peep through the ventilators. Poor Jackson, in whom curiosity sometimes overcame discretion, missed death by an inch at Düren, where a workman hurled a heavy hammer at him as he was looking out. It struck the side of our truck with a crash that made us jump, and although it was difficult to withdraw the head quickly, owing to the narrowness of the opening, Jackson broke the speed record in doing so.

Under other circumstances it would have been galling to cross the Rhine without seeing it and to have passed within a stone's throw of Köln Cathedral without more than a glimpse of a grey stone wall, but by this stage of our journey we were too weak to bother about anything. Even the dirt and stench of our crowded truck had ceased to worry us, although its disgusting condition beggars description, for I can remember only three occasions during the journey on which we were allowed to get out on to the track, and it was not until Saturday morning that we reached our destination, the town of Münster, capital of Westphalia.

The march from the station to our prison camp, some three miles to the south of the town, must have lasted nearly two hours, and it was a distressing experience. We Englishmen and Canadians felt so ill that we had difficulty in getting along, but some Arabs from a French colonial regiment, who had been added to our party, were in a much worse state, for they had all been badly gassed and suffered horribly as they staggered on, coughing and gasping like a flock of exhausted sheep. Goaded forward at bayonet point, prodded with the lances of mounted men when they fell, menaced in their anguish with ruthless revolvers, they were treated as no decent man could treat animals.

To add to our difficulties, one of our party, a man of the Cheshire Regiment, I think, had been shot in the foot and was unable to walk at all, so that the strongest of us had to take turns at carrying him.

It is strange how at times of need there seem to be reserves of energy that can be commanded by the human will, reserves of which one is entirely unconscious until the demand is made. It was just as I was feeling that I could not go any further and wondering what would happen if I copied the Algerians and fell down by the roadside, when I felt a tap on my shoulder and heard the nasal voice of a Canadian asking me to take a turn at carrying this wounded man. On my nodding assent, someone hoisted the poor chap on to my back, and I carried him 'pick-a-back' for the remainder of the journey, a distance of more than half a mile, that seemed at the time to be an infinity.

At last, however, amidst a confusion of shouting guards pushing and bullying, while mounted officers screamed harsh unintelligible orders, our party staggered through some huge wooden gates into the prison *Lager* (camp), which was destined to be my home for nearly eighteen months.

Chapter 3

Lager II, Münster i.W.

After stumbling for some 200 yards along a timbered road, bordered by the tarred backs of wooden barracks, our ragged column straggled under a high covered platform into a huge square. It was completely enclosed by unbroken lines of huts, from the doors of which French prisoners sadly observed us. I was too much occupied with maintaining my relaxing grip upon the legs of the man on my back to notice much, and all I can remember is that I entered one of the barracks, deposited my burden on its dirty floor, and stretched myself half dead with fatigue beside him.

A voice rudely shattered my hopes of rest – '*Vek*! *Raus*! *Rausgehen*! *Englische Schweine*!' Seeing the gleam of a bayonet hovering above my stomach, I rose and limped wearily out into the early sunshine of that inauspicious May Day to join my comrades in the square.

It must have been about 6.00am when coffee and the day's bread ration were served out to us. We felt much better after that and able to enjoy what was perhaps the best feature of the camp, excellent shower baths with hot and cold water. Our clothing was fumigated while we were enjoying this luxury, and then we were free to investigate the bleak geography of the square. We learned that its name was Block IV, and that it formed an exact quarter of the whole prison *Lager* and was capable of accommodating from 2,000 to 3,000 men.

Most of its occupants were Frenchmen, and these crowded about us eager for the latest war news: 'Has Lille been recaptured yet?'

'Is it true that Holland is declaring war on Germany?' 'When is the great English advance to begin?'

Their anxiety regarding Lille was pathetic, for many of them had wives and families in that town at the mercy of its German garrison and had received no news of them since the early days of the war. For the first time in my life I felt glad that I had been taught French on a conversational basis, for I found myself able to pick up the gist of their excited questions and to make some kind of reassuring replies. I remember telling them that England had plenty of men, plenty of money, plenty of ammunitions, and that Deutschland would soon be very thoroughly 'kapoot'.

One little French lad was so gratified by this assurance that he took me to one side, and I sat down with him, our backs against the cook-house in the centre of the block. As soon as we were alone and unobserved, he dived mysteriously into the folds of the voluminous waistband worn by so many of these Frenchmen, and, after much groping, produced two miniature baked potatoes still warm. Poor specimens they were, but we ate them sacramentally while my companion spoke with bated breath of his good fortune in having an '*ami dans la cuisine*' (a friend in the kitchen), who was sometimes able to smuggle titbits to him. Even so, he confessed that he was always '*crevé de faim*' (caving in with hunger), for he was one of the many who received no food parcels from home.

Midday soup created a diversion. It was a nauseating concoction of boiled chestnuts entirely devoid of meat, save for a few grubs and maggots; but, realising the absence of any alternative menu, we made the best of it.

During the afternoon I observed that French prisoners were passing freely in and out of the block entrance, but when I, urged by a desire to explore the whole *Lager*, attempted to leave the block myself, I was rudely turned back by the sentry. So I spent the rest of the day sleeping in the sunshine on the sand outside my barrack room, dreaming of home.

Evening came at last; more 'soup' was issued at 7.00pm – a mixture of hot water and a yellowish powder with an unpleasant and unknown flavour; there was a parade for roll call at 9.00pm and then we were driven into our room for the night.

More like stables than rooms, these barracks were divided by low partitions into alleys, on each side of which ran a layer of improvised mattresses – bags of dusty straw which served us as beds and tables and chairs too, for of other furniture there was none. We did not mind the lack of furniture, but I found the stuffy gloom of these quarters oppressive in the extreme. There was no through-ventilation, the only windows and doors opening on to the desolation of the square, so that when some 200 men had packed themselves sardine fashion in the alleys, the atmosphere soon became fetid. Moreover, the fact that our room happened to be adjacent to the latrine did not help to sweeten it.

I lay awake for long hours during that first night at Rennbahn, my thoughts wandering back to the homeland I had left only a fortnight previously. About me I could hear the heavy breathing of my sleeping companions; from the square came the slow tread of a guard. How long should I have to endure this, I wondered, this buried-alive feeling of suffocation, this helpless inactivity. I wondered whereabouts in Germany I was. We had been allowed to send a postcard home and told that replies were to be addressed:

Kriegsgefangenensendung
Gefangenen Lager II
Münster i.W.

I pondered on the significance of the big word at the top. Münster was evidently the name of the town where we had detrained less than twenty hours ago. What an eternity those twenty hours seemed to be! What did 'i.W.' mean? We could not be far from the Rhine, I thought, for we had passed through Köln on Friday evening and reached Münster very early this morning. It was yesterday evening we were trundling over the Rhine, and our trucks had certainly not travelled at an enormous speed. Yet even a cattle truck can rumble a long way in a few hours. It might be sixty miles to the Rhine, it might be twice that distance. I wondered whether it were possible to escape and whether anyone had ever managed to do so. A noise at the window disturbed my meditation. And there, as if in answer to my question, framed against the glare of the electric lights in the square, I saw the peaked cap of a sentry who was glancing into our room to assure himself that the accursed English were all quiet. We were evidently well watched.

I fell asleep in a mood of black despair.

We were turned out in a drizzling rain at next day to parade for roll call before 'coffee' and our daily bread were issued. At 9.00am there was another parade and we were marched about the square for three hours. This was the daily routine for prisoners who were not employed. The exercise, '*Spaziergang*' or 'promenadey' as we called it, was intended to do us good, to keep us out of mischief and under discipline: yet we hated its monotony, finding it, in our enfeebled condition, wearisome beyond endurance, and men often fainted from the heat and fatigue. It seemed so absurd that all our training as soldiers should end up in this fatuous marching to and fro and round and round in a German prison square. The fact that the French and Russians were compelled to do the same was no consolation, but we were able to gain a little satisfaction from the obvious fact that our

British company was the smartest on the square: we kept step and swung along jauntily, sometimes whistling a tune.

The French marched any old way, a noisy rabblement, some of them trailing along in wooden sabots. As for the Russians – their column had two speeds only, dead slow and stop, shuffling around languidly and painfully, leaving a dust and a stink behind it.

We were glad when this 'promenadey' was over, to find that, since the day was Sunday, midday soup was an improvement on Saturday's concoction. It was turnip water with bits of unknown vegetables in it, and tiny shreds of meat. These bits of meat were bad and gave the whole stuff a rank flavour, but I wished I could have emulated Oliver Twist and asked for more, for I could have consumed six times the quantity. We had to wait until 7.00pm, however, for more, when we were again reminded that the day was Sunday by receiving about three cubic inches of horse flesh in addition to the soup. This meat was a delight to us all, for the English soldier is accustomed to large quantities of meat and, even in so short a time, the change from solid food to what was mainly a soup diet was upsetting our internal organs in an alarming fashion. Possibly the bad meat made us worse. At any rate most of us were very ill for the first few weeks.

My diary for this period reads as follows:

2nd May	Hungry.
3rd May	Bad dinner.
4th May	Diarrhoea. Belgian tells us the war will end in two more months.
5th May	Diarrhoea. Horse beans for dinner.
6th May	Great show of flags – Kaiser's birthday? Ate raw herring. Horrible. Dosed with castor oil and opium. A man dies.
10th May	Sick.
13th May	Very depressed. More French prisoners arrive.
14th May	Still more prisoners arrive.
15th May	Working party leaves the camp.
16th May	Very hungry.

These brief notes need no comment. Time passed with appalling slowness: the first day seemed a week, and the weeks seemed months. We kept up some show of cheerfulness, but at heart most of us were acutely miserable, although we knew that we had less cause for misery than the Russians and most of the French. It was not merely that we were underfed and suffering physically from the wretched quality of what little food we did obtain, but most of us went through periods of severe mental depression, a blend of home sickness and self depreciation, a weariness of body and of mind called by the French *'le cafard'* (literally 'the beetle')! This term, borrowed from the vocabulary of the Foreign Legion, suggested that our trouble resembled the effect of a beetle crawling round in the brain, round and round and round. I envied those among us who were wounded, for I felt that a wound, no matter how slight, mitigated any disgrace attaching to the word surrender, and yet the wounded must have suffered indescribable anguish in those hot, lousy barrack rooms. The worst cases were in special hospital rooms, but we had some fairly bad cases among us.

Skin troubles were common. I developed a most irritating rash, which entirely defeated the simple medical resources of the *Lager*. An English Red Cross man diagnosed it as eczema, but his treatment led to no improvement whatever. The trouble lasted until 1917, long after I had shaken off the dust and lice of Rennbahn, when a little Scot, Dr Stuart, at Wÿnberg Hospital near Cape Town, was finally able to settle the trouble by dosing me with arsenic and calomel and by the application of various ointments.

In spite of all our troubles, life was not entirely devoid of interest. The varied assortment of humanity in that *Lager* would have interested anyone. The place was a Babel. Nowhere on earth can I imagine a greater confusion of tongues. French predominated. There was every possible type of French soldier: solid citizens of Mauberge rubbed shoulders with the sweepings of gutters; simple Bretons mingled with courtly-mannered gentlemen, whose princely gestures and ornate speech seemed to date back to the days before the Revolution; men of the Foreign Legion, Zouaves, and gaily clad Spahis, Arabs from Morocco, full-blooded negroes from Senegal. Browning's description of the variety of rats that followed the Pied Piper comes to my mind as I think of them.

Then there were the Russians. In 1915 the camp must have contained some hundreds of these poor fellows, all in an appalling state of destitution. With no hope at that time of receiving food parcels from anywhere, they were entirely dependent upon German rations and were so weak that many seemed scarcely able to drag themselves about. The less proud among them could be seen at all times wandering disconsolately in the blocks, shiveringly wretched and ill, while

'Rennbahn camp, 1914–17': an illustration (by Rennbahn PoW, Sgt Frank Anderson) from the *Church Times*, May 1917, showing some of the different nationalities imprisoned at Rennbahn.

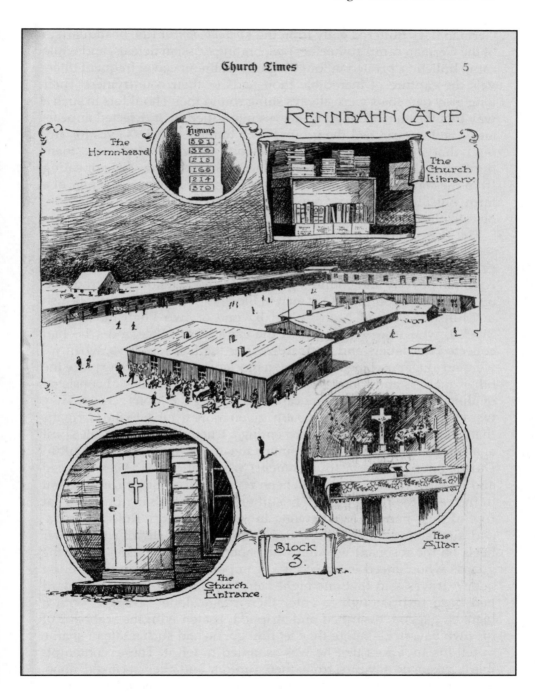

German flags fluttered gaily from the *Kommandantur* (the headquarters of the German camp authorities) celebrating Russian defeats, and while camp bulletins, printed in four languages, announced at frequent intervals the capture of incredible thousands of their countrymen. Their long grey overcoats were always slung round their shoulders in such a way that the empty dangling sleeves intensified their dejected appearance, as they searched the ground with hungry hopeless eyes for any offal that might have escaped previous notice. I often saw them hunting in the refuse tips for the bones or heads of raw fish, or eating from the contents of the swill tubs as they carried them to the pigs at a farm outside the camp. Demoralised and broken, these men were objects of pity in the eyes of all save the most brutal of our guards.

The British company presented some striking contrasts – miners, students, teachers, clerks, men from Canadian forests and from the prairies, rich men, poor men, beggar men, thieves – all reduced to a common poverty and bound together in the good fellowship produced by suffering in common. Our men in Block IV were not the only British in Münster: we had been visited by one or two Englishmen from Block I, who were employed in the camp post office and who had collected our letters and postcards. After the first few days, when we were no longer confined to our own block, we were able to explore the other quarters and found that this other company in Block I consisted of about fifty regular soldiers captured during the Mons retreat. They were a tough lot, and had probably given more trouble to the Germans than all the rest of the camp, presenting a truculent, unbreakable spirit against the most severe disciplinary measures prescribed by Kultur. During periods of *Strafe* (punishment), when rations had been reduced and when several of them had been removed to solitary confinement in the cells, the rest would defy authority by scrambling onto the flat roof of their barrack and bawling in raucous unison 'Rule Britannia' and similar forbidden songs, drumming out the rhythm with their heels on the resonant wooden walls and hurling derisive jeers at the guards who danced in an ecstasy of impotent rage upon the ground below. It was said that one night before our arrival, an armed guard had been rash enough to enter their room alone. Scragged with a blanket, gagged, disarmed and stripped, beaten with the scabbard of his own bayonet – before they let him go, he had such a tale of shame to tell his superiors that he was ashamed to tell it. These 'contemptibles' asked no favours from their captors and they received none. The contempt in which they held their enemies was equalled by their scorn for their French allies, who feared and disliked them, for they demanded precedence in every queue just because they were English soldiers. 'Get out of the sucking way, you b***** old French b*****d!' was their unvarying attitude. The Frenchmen had at first resisted these claims to superiority, but by May 1915 they had learned under the weight of heavy fists the futility of resistance and had decided that the wisest policy for them was to leave these 'Engleesh Tommies' to rule their little corner of the camp in splendid isolation.

Chapter 4

Hunger

We newcomers were not long in settling down among this motley community to a state of what appeared to be patient resignation, a dull grey monotony relieved by occasional gleams of hope that the final victory of the Allies was at hand. We always spoke of peace in a few months – the idea of years in captivity being a torture we refused to contemplate.

The food question remained acute for some weeks, until parcels of provisions began to arrive for us from England towards the end of May. On 10 May I was so weak from hunger that I exchanged my boots for a Frenchman's, receiving four marks as a recognition of the fact that mine were of better quality than his; and with this money I was able to buy from the block canteen a few thin biscuits and a piece of coarse chocolate. The balance I expended on a small tot of rum. This may seem luxurious, but I hoped that, taken to wash down a few quinine tablets I had begged from a French hospital orderly, it might comfort my distressed internal organs. Any benefit that might have resulted from this treatment was, however, entirely annulled two days later by the issue of a ration of raw herring pickled in salt. Although probably considered by the Germans a great delicacy, to most of us it was nauseating beyond description: tough, slimy, acrid with salt, and abominably fishy. Only the direst necessity made us tackle it. Those who could not finish their portion were saved the guilt of waste, for any remnants – heads, tails or bones – thrown out into the square, were immediately scrounged up and devoured by famished Russians, not a particle remaining.

On the next occasion that fish was introduced into our diet, Hesborough, a man of the Suffolk regiment, more squeamish and more daring than the rest of us, made a fire in the square, and very soon we were all copying his example. Lack of fuel presented a difficulty, but one or two loose planks were soon torn up from the floor of our room, and in no time some twenty little spirals of blue smoke began to rise peacefully in the evening twilight, each tended by one or two ravenous but happy men who were toasting their herrings on wooden spits and on the points of knives or grilling them over the hot embers on bits of bent wire. The savoury smell of the cooking fish, mingling sweetly with the aromatic wood smoke, afforded us the most pleasurable sensations imaginable. At first the Germans were too thunderstruck to do more than gape. But this inactivity on their part was much too good to last. After a few minutes, yells of rage from the direction of the guard room warned us that the source of our wood supply had been announced to the *Feldwebel* (German sergeant-major) in charge of our block. And then down upon us there charged the guard, a dozen stout Germans with fixed bayonets and heavy boots. Most of us, hastily grabbing our half-cooked fish, ignominiously bolted. Hesborough and one or two others of more heroic fibre, who stayed to argue, found argument unavailing against boot and bayonet and were ruthlessly rolled over among the scattered brands of their own fires, their fish knocked out of their hands and stamped into the dust. In no time our fires had all been trampled out, and we were shut up in our rooms to discuss the vileness of the German character and to wish that we had the means of exterminating the entire breed. True, save for bruises and an odd bayonet scratch, none of us was hurt, but some had lost their fish, and all had suffered the ignominy of defeat; and if forceful language and bitter hate could blast anything at all, the whole of Germany would have shrivelled that night in the flame that dieth not.

It was sometime during this early period of semi-starvation that further tribulation was heralded among us by the distribution of small rectangular cards each ruled off into six or eight spaces and each headed in block capitals with the sinister looking word '*Impfung*' (vaccination). The spaces on these cards were all labelled with the name of some serious disease – smallpox, typhoid, cholera, and the like – and we wondered what they signified. It was not long before we knew, for on 17 May we newcomers were all marched out of Block IV, up the Lagerstrasse into Block I, to parade outside the hospital there, our cards in our hands. In a short time the hospital door opened, and we were ordered to enter in single file. It was a big room with beds round its sides, and at its far end our queue passed slowly round a table spread with syringes and basins, where two German medical officers were sitting. As each man approached this table, he bared his chest to be dabbed by an orderly with some solution or other; and then one of the doctors jabbed a hypodermic needle into him. After this, one moved round in the queue to another table, where each man's card was stamped by a German orderly in the appropriate space to certify that he had been well and truly 'impfunged'. Then we were free to return to Block IV.

I felt very uneasy about this 'impfunging' business. The idea of having any kind of bugs, alive or dead, squirted under my skin was always an abomination to me, even when the operation was performed by an English medico – and what ungodly filth these fat Huns were experimenting with, we had no idea. They probably meant well, I thought, but they looked an ugly pair of brutes. How could we be certain that they did mean well? There were several more stamps required on my card, and before I dozed off to sleep that night on my dirty old straw bag, I cogitated for a long time upon the problem of how to get that card fully stamped without undergoing any more 'impfunging', but I could see no way of doing so.

To my horror we were marched off to the hospital again the following afternoon. Again we saw the glittering array of bottles and lancets. As the front end of our file reached the doctors and we were ordered to bare our arms, I saw it was to be a vaccination this time. I had been vaccinated less than a year previously, but what would be the use of telling that tale? The thought of two sets of bugs at work in my blood at the same time filled me with dismay – for I was feeling sore and seedy as the result of the previous day's treatment – and I looked round feverishly for some avenue of escape. The line of men who had been vaccinated was only a few yards from those who like myself were moving forwards to the doctors, and suddenly the solution of the difficulty occurred to me. Seizing a favourable moment, I stepped quickly and lightly across this space, turning my back upon the altar of sacrifice and joining the queue at the stamping table. I thus made a circuit which cut out the lancets and the lymph. My card duly stamped, I emerged triumphant, feeling that I had scored over the Hun and his system and that 'impfunging' would never again cause me any uneasiness. Unfortunately, I was never able to repeat my little manoeuvre, for someone was caught in the act of copying it, and on later occasions the stamping table was so placed that any short circuiting was impossible.

Heaven only knows how many filthy cultures were pumped into our scraggy bodies during this inoculation period, and some of us were very ill as a result. However, letters began to come from the Homeland at about this time to give us much needed consolation, and these were soon followed by our first parcels.

No one without actual experience of a war prison can possibly appreciate the significance of these first parcels of English food or realise the bitter disappointment of those of us who received none. The deliveries were made at an office in the Lagerstrasse, from which an English sergeant called out the names of the fortunate at a given hour. My diary records that the first batch of parcels for those who had reached Rennbahn on May Day were issued on 19 May, and this distribution was followed by several others during the week. I remember that it was my fate during that week to be numbered among those who waited outside the office in vain, and my need of food was so great that I sold my puttees to a Frenchman for 3 marks and spent that sum on the coarse chocolate, which was the sole edible obtainable at the canteen. I was in sore straits, for my skin was covered with sores, and I felt that unless I could supplement the rations with some kind of real food I should die. I must have looked pretty ill, for I remember Hesborough, the great-hearted Suffolk man, giving me a large chunk of English cake. Poor old Hesborough! He will never know the warmth of gratitude with which, even after these sixteen years, I still recall that generous gift; he was drafted away in June on a working party and we heard a few months later that he had been killed by the guards for refusing to work in a mine.

Riach of the Durhams is another whom I shall never forget. It was he who, after receiving a couple of good food parcels, gave me most of his German ration on top of my own for several successive days.

I believe that these two men really saved my life.

It was not long, however, before I received a parcel myself. A delivery had been announced for the afternoon of 27 May. It was a dismal day and a large crowd of us had stood under a drizzling rain in the Lagerstrasse for an hour or more, when suddenly I heard the stentorian voice of the parcels sergeant yell out my own name. Pushing through my envious comrades and mounting the two or three wooden steps which led into the office, I found myself before a long counter on to which prisoners on the postal staff were lifting parcels of all shapes and sizes. Standing behind the counter were two German soldiers, whose duty it was to open and censor each package as it was claimed. I saw my own bit of property on the counter as soon as I entered, recognising my father's writing on the label, and my heart sank as I noticed how badly it had been crushed: bits of broken wood poked their ends through a tangle of string and tatters of brown paper, and I had a glimpse of English bread inside it. 'Kapoot!' ejaculated the perspiring censor as he cut the string and allowed the fragments which had once been a wooden box to fall to the counter. Alas! He was right. Two loaves of bread he lifted out, yellow and green with mould, rotten throughout and stinking; and although I stretched out my hands for them in the hope that some portion might be edible, the German dropped them regretfully into a waste bin. He shook his head and I felt his sympathy as we peered together into the debris remaining – a sticky mess of butter that had been melted and squashed and had gone rancid, all mixed up with bits of broken chocolate and fragments of glass from what had once been a small jar of honey. The censor gingerly fished out a small tin of oxo cubes from this mixture and sighed as he let the rest slide in one sticky tangle into the bin. '*Nix goot*!' he said and I left the office with my oxo cubes, sick at heart.

My dejection was not of long duration, for I found that an oxo cube was a very welcome addition to the soup ration and that tiny bits of oxo eaten with German bread made even that sour concoction quite appetising. Moreover, on the following day I had another parcel – tinned tongue, some lemon curd, and a small cake making up for another mouldy loaf which completed its contents – and on 1 June three more came for me all together. From then onwards I received two or three every week with very rare exceptions and, generally speaking, almost every Englishman in the camp was always possessed of some English food to supplement his meagre soup and bread.

Bread usually arrived in bad condition during the hot weather of 1915, but later on our friends at home learned better ways of making it and packing it and the supply improved. We found that it was unwise to eat mouldy bread, those of us who managed to sneak a bad loaf past the censor usually suffering severe stomach ache as the result.

The amount of food that came from England astonished the guards. They read in their newspapers that England was starving, and yet here before their eyes was food galore arriving from the land of famine; food, too, that was very much superior to their own scant rations. They eyed it hungrily enough, poor beggars.

We received, practically speaking, every parcel posted to us at Rennbahn. Nothing seemed to be stolen on the railway journey from Holland. Of course, we prisoners took them from the trucks ourselves, fatigue parties man-hauling them in carts from Hiltrup, the nearest station. The German censors never opened one except in its owner's presence. Men who were sent from the *Lager* 'on *Kommando*' were not so fortunate. Their parcels often went astray.

Chapter 5

Camp Activities and Amusements

The effect upon us of a little good food was felt immediately. Cheered in mind and strengthened in body, we began to make the best we could of the period in exile. Amusements of all kinds were taken up, and there were times when our block looked like a comparatively happy kind of rest camp.

I still retain mental pictures of tranquil summer afternoons in 1915. In one corner the sun is beating down on a group of men round a 'Crown and Anchor' board, from another come strident cries which announce the progress of the English soldiers' favourite game – 'House'; here are a couple of men immersed in a chess match, there a couple of draught enthusiasts; in the Querstrasse, the Western cross road of the *Lager* where a court has been marked out, immaculate French adjutants may be seen enjoying a game of tennis.

Actually, for those who received enough parcels and had money and who could forget the humiliating futility of captivity, life at Rennbahn was far from devoid of pleasure. The wearisome 'exercise' was cut down after a few months and finally abandoned altogether. A camp library supplied us with an excellent selection of books – French, English, German and Russian.

We even had a theatre. This theatre was at first run entirely by the French, being directed by a member of the Paris Conservatoire. Among its actors were professionals from the Parisian stage; scenery was made and painted in the camp by men who in civil life had been joiners and artists; good dresses were hired from German firms; lighting was satisfactory, and I can remember seeing some first-rate plays during my exile in Germany. *L'Abbé Constantin*, *Le Chemineau* and *Mon bebé* were especially memorable productions, and indeed most of the shows attained so high a degree of perfection that it was possible for us 500 or 600 men in the audience to forget the German censor in the front row and the armed guards at the door, possible even to lose ourselves so completely in sheer enjoyment as to forget that we were captives, for these French productions would have done credit to any company of actors in the world.

Then there were French concerts, brass and woodwind too. It was at Rennbahn that I heard my first symphony concert.

Not long after our arrival, we English began to form organisations of our own. The church came first and the growth of the Rennbahn Church was very interesting. There were three English-speaking Protestant clergymen who visited Rennbahn – Olandt, Fladd and Williams. Olandt, an American, was the only one of the three that I ever remember meeting, for their visits were infrequent, but I believe it was a visit from Pastor Williams that inspired a drummer, V.C. Campon of the E. Lancs, who had been a lay reader in the Church of England, to obtain permission to hold English services on Sunday mornings in the theatre. He tried to make these services of such a nature as to agree with every possible shade of Christian theology, and for a time they were well attended. He was an energetic fellow, and, assisted by a few friends, organised some English concerts in an effort to pay small expenses connected with the church. He hired an American organ from a Münster firm and obtained a number of hymn books and bibles from sympathisers at home. After a while his Church of England bias showed itself, and as the novelty of the camp services wore off, the number of the faithful steadily diminished.

Then there arose the time-honoured dispute as to church control. Was it to remain an autocracy? Was it to become democratic?

A gathering storm of criticism of Drummer Campon finally burst on 25 July, when, by permission of the German authorities, a public meeting was called by the senior British NCO, a sergeant piper of the Royal Scots. It was only the genial chairmanship of this old pipe major that saved the meeting from becoming an undignified slanging match, but before it had dispersed, a democratic and nondenominational church committee was elected, with the pipe major as its permanent chairman and Dr Campon as its secretary. After this, events moved apace. To support church expenses, a sub-committee was appointed to run a series of British concerts, and on 7 August this body broke away from its parent and gave itself the imposing title 'The Rennbahn British Social Club'.

In addition to concerts, football matches and boxing contests were arranged. Small charges were made for admission to these events, or collections were taken, and after the payment of church expenses, the balance profit was handed over to the *Caisse de Secours*. (The *Caisse de Secours* was a 'Helping Fund' originated by the French for the relief of necessitous prisoners of all nationalities. It was maintained partly by the profits of their own theatrical and orchestral entertainments and partly by subscriptions in money and in kind from France.)

Campon did not like the idea of the church receiving its income from a 'Social Club', and in response to his urge for independence, a magazine, the *Rennbahn Church Times*, made its appearance on 22 September, with the drummer as its editor and myself as his sub.

What a job we had in turning out a hundred copies of this every month! After collecting our articles, we did the first stage of the printing on a typewriter hired in Münster, then we inked over each typed letter with a special ink, and finally each page was transferred on to a gelatine pad from which as many copies as possible were printed. We got a French artist, M. Lacombe, to do our first cover designs, and before the end of the year an English artist, named Anderson, who had been captured in October, lent his aid. Thanks to Anderson's skill and generous help, the appearance of our magazine improved rapidly, and the success with which copies were sold enabled the church to pay its small expenses without much more help from the Social Club.

I had some misgivings at this time as to the wisdom of allowing copies of our periodical to reach England, for I feared that they might give too rosy an impression of prison life and lead readers to imagine the German treatment of war captives was a model for humanity. But my fears were groundless, the Christmas number of the paper being reproduced and sold in Durham in 1916 in an effort to raise money for the aid of prisoners of war.

Our worthy church secretary continued to work indefatigably. He started a Bible class before the close of 1915, and then, early in 1916, since it seemed scarcely fitting that services should be held in the theatre, he persuaded Herr General von Steinecke to allow part of a large store room in Block IV to be partitioned off and converted into a respectable church.

It was Eddie Hinks, a great, bearded Canadian, who undertook to make benches and other furniture that was required. The Germans supplied the timber. Eddie was a taciturn kind of chap, but I remember how he once felt moved to make some kind of apology for tackling so sacred a task: 'I've no goddarn use for bawling hymns and pestering the Almighty with prayers,' he told me, 'but if the poor guys that go in for that kind of thing want a few bits of furniture knocking together, I guess I'm the boy to do it.' The searing blasphemies he uttered while at work would have brought tears to the eyes of the average English churchgoer, but he made a grand job of the church furniture.

The keen interest taken in the establishment of some kind of religious organisation in the camp came, I suppose, from a genuine desire on the part of some men to satisfy deep spiritual needs. Yet, although there was none of what in times of peace is designated 'Religion for Respectability's sake', there were more reasons than one for the formation of a church in Rennbahn.

I remember a great argument held in our alley during the church furnishing period. Heeling, a Nonconformist of the ascetic type, a man of burning sincerity and caustic tongue, was expressing his views to Banford, a studious well-read fellow of gentle disposition. 'What Campon wanted,' he said vehemently, his face expressive of utter scorn, 'is a soft job that would keep him safe from fatigues and working parties for the duration. And he's got it. The man is an out and out hypocrite.'

Corporal Ramwell, one of the circle, interrupted, laying a hand on the speaker's arm. 'Hold on a bit!' he said in a placating tone. 'He is not the only man that is glad of a soft job. I reckon we are all after that. And if our church secretary thinks he can cut work by holding prayer meetings, good luck to him! What's the harm in it? As for hypocrisy, I think you're wrong. He believes what he preaches and sees a need for what he calls religion. It isn't your sort of religion nor mine, but he is sincere enough.'

'Then why the devil!' (we gasped, for this was a shocking expression coming from Heeling) – 'why does he shave the hair off his forehead, and wear window-glass pince-nez? Why does he style himself "Dr", and let people who don't know it stands for "drummer" think he's a doctor? And why does he write his initials after instead of before his name? Dr Campon, V.C.! If he dare do it, I tell you, he would write "Bishop of Rennbahn" after it as well.' There was a world of contempt in the speaker's voice.

Banford had listened to this tirade with a tolerant smile. Now he turned a thoughtful face to me. 'A bit rough on our worthy pastor, isn't he? It does seem a pity that our secretary lays himself open so unnecessarily to criticism. He does not get much out of a pose that everyone sees through. But I agree with Ramwell that the chap is sincere enough in his way. Perhaps he thinks folks at home will be more impressed if he signs himself Dr, and puts his initials last, more inclined to help on the good work with subs and so on.'

A raucous Canadian oath rasped out. The long loose-limbed figure of Hayntree had pushed into the circle: he was an avowed agnostic and freethinker. 'Guess I'm through with the whole stinking bunch of psalm-singin' bible punchers! What good do you reckon you do with all your suckin' prayers? There are all the Germans prayin' away for favours to be given to them and for our fellows to be blown to hell. If there's a God Almighty, it seems he will have a job to know which side is squealin' the hardest. There's only one religious guy in the whole *Lager* I give two cents for, and that's the bleedin' old nigger that mucks in with the little Gurks. He looks like knowin' more than all your church committees put together.'

We were all silent for a moment, thinking of the man he referred to. He was a huge, bearded Sikh, the most solitary and striking figure in the camp. He spoke to nobody. His majestic dignity was such that even our guards seemed to respect him. Every morning at sunrise we saw him kneeling alone in a quiet portion of the block to begin the day with prayer and meditation. Then Banford spoke again: 'He seems to have his own window through which to see God. But leaving him out of it, and leaving Campon out of it, I see a jolly good reason for having a Christian service together once a week. Somehow it's a link with home.' He faltered a little as though half-ashamed to utter the word which lay so near our hearts. 'It's good to be able to do something that they are doing over there, at the same time, in the same way.'

I noticed a smouldering impatience in Hayntree's expression and tried to speak soothingly. 'If singing a few hymns together once or twice a week helps to keep us cheery, let us have them. There's a good deal in what Banford says and, although I hate humbug, I am going to stick by old man Campon and see if he can't do some practical good through his organisation. Anyway, the more cushy jobs we can invent, the fewer men will be left for German work parties. You fellows can argue about dogmas and theology if you like.'

Our church and all our British activities were the focus of great interest among the French, our boxing contests and exhibitions especially. These attracted great crowds from every quarter of the camp, for we had among us several good regimental boxers and, best of all, a champion middle-weight named Coucher, who had at one time been one of Carpentier's sparring partners and who could make rings round any other exponent of the noble art in the camp. In appearance the very personification of ruthless power, this professional fighter was really the soul of gentle good nature, encouraging even the most timid youngsters to spar with him and putting all his knowledge of boxing at our service. He has probably quite forgotten me, but I shall never forget him, nor the lessons I enjoyed from him. Above all, I remember the occasion on which I almost knocked him out, and the hiding he gave me afterwards.

We had donned the gloves in one of the English barrack rooms, and he taunted me with my inability to hit him. I had directed blow after blow into the midst of his derisive grin only to find my glove landing in empty space, with the grin persisting an inch or two below or to the side of it, while my room mates roared their appreciation. The more they laughed the more desirous of hitting him I became, and when he turned his head to speak to one of these spectators, giving me a momentary glimpse of the corner of his jaw bone just below the ear, the temptation was too great for me. 'Thud' – my blow landed. To my surprise, for I never dreamed that I could hurt him badly, the colossus reeled and staggered backwards. There was a sudden silence in the room.

'Got you that time, anyway!' I said cheerfully, and then I saw his face and my cheerfulness evaporated. It was a sinister face I scarcely recognised, a face that only his professional opponents ever saw – eyes steely through horizontal slits, the mouth set in an ugly line, cruel, merciless.

'You young bastard!' he hissed. 'Come on!'

Of the ensuing ten seconds my memory is confused, but I think the first thing I lost was some of the skin of my nose stroked off with a sweep downward of his gloves, and then came the deluge.

'Give him a dog's, Albert!' I heard someone cry nervously, as I was driven backwards under what seemed a rain of blows from which there was no escaping. Then a pile of bedding behind me tripped my heels and over I went, thanking all the powers that be for the respite. It was more than a respite. I realised it was the end, for I saw the good-humoured grin had returned to the champion's face as he bent down and pulled me to my feet.

'You nearly knocked me out!' he laughed. 'You asked for some sucking trouble, and I reckon you got it!'

And I had, but I knew he had let me off lightly, for if but one of his punches had carried any weight of malice behind it, this book would never have been written. As it was, I lost nothing but some skin and a little blood from lips and nose, not even a tooth being loosened. He explained later that the corner of the jaw was a most dangerous spot to land a heavy blow and demonstrated this truth by tapping me on it with one of his fingers. I was surprised at the effect and ceased to marvel that I had hurt him. I enjoyed many more lessons in boxing, but never again have I hit a professional hard when he was not looking.

Our French allies agreed that our boxing was magnificent, but we had to acknowledge that our theatrical performances were crude as compared with their finished and artistic programmes. Their numerical superiority gave them an advantage, and I think the French temperament suits the stage better than ours does. Moreover, their actors were less liable to be sent away from the *Lager* on working parties, '*Kommandos*', than our men, for many of their chief artistes were NCOs exempt from work, whereas all our organisations were in constant danger of being broken up by the sudden removal of important members to farms or mines or factories anywhere in Germany.

Chapter 6

Work

The officer in charge of our *Lager*, a General Herr von Steinecke, was a portly, white-moustached old gentleman, who obviously bore us no special ill will and who was especially kind to the French. Perhaps rumour was correct that he had a son a prisoner in France. He occasionally visited the French theatre, where his nods, his beaming smiles and his genial manner indicated the height of enjoyment; and I remember at least one attendance he made at an English performance, which also appeared to delight him. By comparing accounts of other German prisons with my own knowledge of Rennbahn, I have concluded that ours, while under the command of Herr von Steinecke, was one of the best in the country.

Unfortunately, it was merely a central camp from which labour could be continually supplied to German industry, so that, of the thousands of prisoners who entered it, only a very small percentage enjoyed its comparative comfort for more than a month or two before being sent away on some working party or other. All prisoners loathed the idea of working for the enemy. Whatever we did was bound to liberate Germans for the fighting services: even agricultural labour supplied food, most of which was destined ultimately to conversion into energy aimed at the destruction of our own people. This same reason which made us loathe work inspired the Germans with a desperate anxiety to get every possible ounce of work out of us, and it was the conflict between these two opposing points of view that led to so much brutality and which bred in the hearts of most prisoners of war a hatred of Germany, which survives even to this day.

Some heroic souls among us flatly refused to work, but this was a course which usually led to very severe punishment. '*Nix Arbeit, nix Essen*' (No work, no food), expressed one unanswerable line of action adopted to meet refractory cases; and there were other still more drastic means of persuasion known to the guards on *Kommandos*, compared to which our British Field Punishment No. 1 was merely a gentle correction.

Some of us managed to evade industrial work by obtaining employ-ment in the *Lager*. Although there was not a single prisoner in the camp who felt absolutely secure from the threat of *Kommando*, the men employed in the bank and the post office were fairly safe, as were the tailors (one or two large rooms in the *Lager* were used as tailors' shops, where a large number of French prisoners worked. What kind of clothes they made, I never found out) and cooks and canteen keepers. Sergeants were of course exempt from actual work. I remember one bright Frenchman who happened, in the early days just after his arrival, to obtain a few yards of gold braid which he made into chev-rons, so that he was able to promote himself and some of his friends to the rank of adjutant, thus saving them a great deal of trouble. Most of us, however, found compromise the wisest and best course. We feigned intense stupidity; we slacked with clear consciences, doing as little as possible as badly as ever we could.

In May and early June my own experiences of work were confined to camp fatigues, and I recall one or two excursions I was compelled to make round Block IV, sweeping and spearing bits of paper and refuse on an instrument that was a cross between a long toasting fork and a toy lance and then wheeling the rubbish away in a handcart. I did not like it, but one or two mornings spent in the block kitchen cleaning potatoes for the soup were still more detestable, for the spuds were bad and stinking. On 23 June, however, I was paraded with a half score of other Britishers and marched off to work in a brickyard close to the camp.

That brickyard experience was delightful. On arriving, we were directed to convey new bricks from the kilns and to stack them near the road for carting away. We began to work very slowly, trundling our loads with infinite care over the lines of planks which bridged the miry clay of the yard and pretending to be too weak to control them. The old manager, or owner, watched us for a time and then, as the work seemed to be proceeding satisfactorily, he left us in the charge of our guards and shuffled away. No sooner had he affected his depar-ture than we diverted the course of our stream of barrows, building up a beautiful stack of bricks as far away from the right spot as possible. The manager's rage upon his return an hour or so later was glorious to behold. Unfortunately, except for Kohn, an anglicised Jew who had been captured with us, we were all ignorant of the German tongue, so that we lost much of the significance of the harsh sounding words that poured in a continuous stream from his wide mouth; Kohn, however, shook with what the old manager probably thought was fear, but which we knew to be suppressed delight, and the rest of us wished we could share it.

We soon got busy again, laboriously removing our stack into its right place, the German watching us intently the while, muttering to himself and sometimes floundering along beside us, emitting sundry grunts and snorts of indignation.

All went well for a short time, and then one of us had an accident. His barrow wheel slipped from the plank, and in a moment its load of clean new bricks was upset into the mud, so that traffic was dislocated for ten minutes or more. This gave us an idea, and after that we took turns in having accidents – the climax being reached when two barrows were upset together. This was too much for the manager. Unable to keep still, he was standing first on one foot, then on the other, beside himself and looking half strangled in an ecstasy of passion; his bald dome of head and his purple face streamed with sweat, and the corded veins in his neck threatened to burst as he gasped out volleys of guttural abuse.

'What's the old son of a bitch working his jaws about, Kohn?' growled Ellis, an imperturbable Canadian. 'Tell him to put a sock in his potato masher.'

Kohn was making obvious attempts to soothe him. He told us afterwards that he had explained to the old gentleman how unreasonable it was of him to expect us to learn brick-making in an hour or two, that we were doing our best, that he must give us time. But his efforts were futile; the spate of wrath continued. The guards were appealed to – would they make us work properly, *'faule Schweine,'* (*faul* = lazy) *'verdammte Engländer'* that we were? But the guards chanced to be genial young soldiers who were obviously enjoying the show; they made deprecatory gestures, shrugging their shoulders as they explained that they were there as escorts, not as slave drivers. What could they do? Finally, after an hour or so more, during which time we enjoyed ourselves like a company of mischievous schoolboys, the manager reached the end of his tether and the limit of his vocabulary. Throwing up his podgy hands as though to invoke help from above, he screamed to the guards to take us away, and back we marched to the *Lager* never to work in that brickyard again.

In some German camps we would have been punished by curtailment of rations and eight or ten hours of standing to attention in the barrack yard. In others we would have been clubbed and beaten. But at Rennbahn under the rule of von Steinecke nothing was done to us at all.

I sometimes wonder what happened under similar circumstances to German prisoners in allied countries; but I cannot imagine any Germans acting as we did. We were awkward people to handle, seeing no reason for gratitude that our lives had been spared on the battle-field, merely to be worn out by slow starvation or broken on the wheel of German industry. We could seldom forget that our guards were our enemies, and though in our hearts we knew some of them to be kindly men, we refused to acknowledge it. For the most part we hated them. We hated them as we watched them swelling their great paunches with beer and smoking their long wooden pipes on their bench outside the block guardroom; we hated them as we heard their heavy monot-onous tread around the camp at night time. To see them was to hate them. And most of them hated us too.

But this was war.

We as soldiers could see only one side. We might have thought of the guards as men exiled like ourselves from families they loved, scarred like ourselves with the wounds of war, calloused by a military training more harsh than ours, burdened by more serious economic anxiety. We might have seen the choleric brickyard manager in another light – an old man trying in the face of great difficulties to carry on his business, hampered by war restrictions, bereft of his sons, struggling bravely to make ends meet and to do his bit for the beloved *Vaterland*. But he was our enemy, one of the accursed Huns; the guards were Huns; it was our business to hate and be hated. The war would have ceased if hate had died. To understand is to forgive even the hatred.

After my day in the brickyard, I was saved from the necessity of ever doing any more work for our captors by being appointed 'British Rep-resentative on the Central Committee of the *Caisse de Secours*'. It was Stanley Webb, a Londoner whose regiment I have forgotten [Private Stanley Webb of the 8th Middlesex], to whom I was really indebted for this piece of good fortune. He came over to me one day towards the end of June as I sat on my bed talking to a French acquaintance, and expressed surprise at my knowledge of the language. 'You are just the man Allée is looking for!' he exclaimed with enthusiasm.

He told me that Allée was the senior French adjutant, that he lived in Block III, that he was the president of the *Caisse de Secours*, and that he was trying to cement the Entente Cordiale by finding an English-man who knew the French language and making him a member of that committee.

'What about yourself?' I asked. 'You could do that job as well as I could.'

But he brushed this suggestion aside, 'I don't know enough of the dashed lingo. May I recommend you as a suitable man?'

Needless to say, I gratefully assented and later on in the day, Webb came to me again to tell me that we were invited to have tea with the president that afternoon. I realised that I was to be inspected, but the suggestion of food consoled me, and at 4.00pm we wandered into Block III.

We found M. Allée luxuriating in a deck chair outside his room, engrossed in a copy of Edna Lyall's *Donovan*, a small, alert, sturdily built man with swarthy skin and active dark eyes. He rose to greet us, displaying that charm and courtesy which characterises the educated Frenchman the world over, and expressing in fluent English his delight at seeing us. As we entered his barrack we were astonished to hear him apologise for its crowded condition. It contained about a score only of rough wooden bedsteads; facing south and bathed in sunshine, it seemed delightfully airy and bright after the gloom of our own congested quarters.

We two guests occupied stools while the Frenchman sitting on his bed gave us his views on recent English literature. I should have enjoyed his talk under different circumstances, but, as it was, I fear my attention continually wandered to his batman bending over a tin on the stove, and I speculated on what viands might be put before us. Webb confessed afterwards that his mind had been similarly divided. We were looking forward to this meal, for English parcels had been held up for a few days and we were hungry. At last the man left the stove and placed a board over our host's bed, spreading a blue table cloth over it. Ye gods! – a table-cloth in Rennbahn! Then three real cups and saucers appeared, the first we had seen since leaving England.

Things looked rosy.

'Ze faive o'clock,' smiled our host, as his batsman poured a bluish green fluid from an improvised saucepan into the cups and then set down a small tin of thin arrowroot biscuits.

I realised that the feast was now spread, and endeavouring to conceal my disappointment, sipped the 'tea' with as much show of appreciation as I could muster. Although well boiled, it was very weak and, being unsweetened and devoid of milk, could scarcely be called a delicious beverage. However, we ate as many biscuits as decency permitted – perhaps more than that – thanked our host for his kindness, and departed with the assurance that I should speedily be nominated as a member of the French committee and should henceforth be exempt from all working parties and fatigues.

The 'staff appointment' came just in time, for on 2 July, a party of some 200 British were told to leave Rennbahn for agricultural work.

They assembled in the square – a jolly crowd – many of them looking forward to a change from the dreary monotony and bleak ugliness of the *Lager*; one might escape from a farm; and anyway starvation would be impossible among orchards and grain fields; there would be rabbits too, and perhaps an occasional hare, eggs, even chickens if the gods were kind. So they were all in good spirits as they stood with their small bundles of personal property, and, waiting for orders to move off, cracking profane jokes at the expense of their guards and whistling snatches from old songs.

Conspicuous among them was Jack Billson, still bandaged about the neck where a bullet had scored a deep groove in April. He stood half a head above most of his comrades, as big and burly as ever, despite the hardships of prison life, cheery and good humoured. With him were one or two others of my own special pals – Hattick, the man who had shared with me the morsel of green vegetable he had found in the truck that brought us to Münster, and Riach who had been able to give me extra soup in those early days when even a crust of mouldy bread was a luxury.

'Cheerio!' boomed Billson's jolly voice, as the party tramped across the block towards the Lagerstrasse. 'We'll send you some rabbits soon.'

'Ay, and don't forget a few Turkeys for Christmas, Jack!'

The *Lager* seemed lonely without these old friends; some of us wished we had volunteered to accompany them, for farming, even on German land, seemed pleasant in comparison with life in our dirty, lousy barracks, shut off almost entirely from all sights and sounds of the country. We pictured Billson and the rest of them working among fragrant fields of hay or harvesting later on. Possibly very soon some of them would seize some opportunity of legging it and getting back to England. We almost envied them.

It was on Saturday, 17 July, that we heard a rumour of Billson's return to Rennbahn. I had just finished giving a lesson in English to a French sergeant and was crossing the block on my return to my room, when I met Hicky, the British librarian, who was bubbling over with the news.

'Old Billson's in clink (clink = soldier's word for prison cell) in Block II,' he shouted.

I was sceptical, for rumour in a prison camp maintained its reputation as a lying jade, but Hicky insisted.

'It's right enough! I got it from Ramwell in the Post Office. Let's go into Block II and see what we can find out.'

I had no hope of seeing him, for a man in the cells was completely isolated from the rest of us and Block II was the abode of mystery at all times, for we were seldom allowed to enter it, and it was used mainly for stores and for the temporary accommodation of newcomers. However, a little bluff went a long way in a prison camp, and we walked towards the entrance of Block II with all the assurance of inspecting officers.

'Halt!' shouted the sentry at the entrance, the business end of his bayonet threatening Hicky's stomach. It was useless for Hicky to seize the opportunity of airing his German and to explain that he wished to see the Corporal Billson. The guard was adamant. We had to retreat.

We had a glimpse of him a few days later, as we peered in through the block entrance, but again the sentry ordered us away, and it was a week or two before he emerged from the unknown and rejoined us in Block IV. My diary gives the day of his return as Wednesday 11 August, and I remember how he came in among us just as Hicky and Webb and Eddie Hinks were hunting up some food for 'tea'. He was haggard and pale, with a strained anxious look in his eyes, and it was some time before we could get him to talk about his experiences. What a story it was!

The agricultural party that had left us so cheerfully on 2 July had been taken by train from Münster into the heart of industrial Westphalia, and after a journey of a couple of hours, had left the train and been marched through jeering crowds along the streets of a big town, which they discovered to be Dortmund, and lodged in barracks in a barbed-wire compound nearby to a huge coal mine with by-product works. Quarters were clean and airy, and except for a shortage of blankets, conditions were more comfortable than in Rennbahn; the food was slightly more generous too.

The day after their arrival, the prisoners were marched into the by-product works and employed in feeding ovens and filling wagons. There were hundreds of prisoners of varied nationality employed in the mine and about it, all of them on twelve-hour shifts. Individuals who stood out and refused to work were knocked about and ill-treated and starved until their resistance was broken down. Work went on continuously for seven days in the week and every other Sunday; night and day shifts were changed round by the simple expedient of making the day-shift continue for a second period of twelve hours without a break.

Billson told us the story very simply.

'We worked for a week without any fuss,' he said. 'Then on Sunday, 11 July, after doing our usual day-shift from 6.00am to 6.00pm, instead of being allowed to turn in to bed when we had eaten the usual evening soup, we were ordered to go on night-shift immediately. Our hands were raw with shovelling, our feet swollen and sore with standing on hot coke, and we were about as tired as fumes and gases and a week's unremitting hard labour could make us. We protested against this twenty-four hour stretch, refusing to turn out. Then the guards rushed in, prodding us with bayonets, striking us with rifle butts and driving us out into the coke yard. It happened to be a wet night and we were told we could stand there soaking until we were willing to work. Some sat down in the mud, only to be prodded and kicked on to their feet again. The weather became worse. We were too tired to speak and felt like broken-down horses on a cab-stand as the rain hissed down upon us, glistening in the light of the great arc lamps. An hour or two had gone by, when suddenly a man stepped out and said he would rather get warm working than stand and shiver all night long, and he was soon followed by others, all of us giving in eventually. We made a show of working until next morning, when the 6 o'clock buzzer released us to find rest in our hammocks.'

We got the rest of the story out of him by degrees. Being a corporal, he had felt some responsibility in regard to his companions, and on the evening of the 12th, just before the time to go on night-shift, he had climbed on to a box and done a bit of stump oratory, urging his fellows to hang together in a definite refusal to do any more work whatever in either coke yard or mine, on the grounds that hours were unreasonable and the work not suitable for prisoners of war. The result of his speech was that a large number of men agreed to strike, and, notwithstanding threats and blows and the menace of bayonet points, some 200 men refused to leave their barrack room that night. Next day, Tuesday, 13 July, several men were dragged out into the yard and beaten, and Billson, as NCO in charge, protested violently against this brutality, explaining his point of view through a Belgian interpreter and demanding that the questions of the legality of the hours and conditions of their work be submitted to a higher authority; but his protest had no effect whatever. Food was curtailed; the men were told that they should receive no more parcels or letters until they resumed work and, that if they persisted in their attitude, they should be sent to work in punishment camps among the marshes of Hannover; every argument that could be thought of was used to break down their resistance. By Thursday there were still sixty men holding out, and since no brutality seemed to shake their resolution, they were marched to the station, en route, for all they knew, to the Hanoverian marshes. They were surprised and relieved when they found themselves again at Münster and were marched up to their old *Lager* for internment in Block II. On Friday, 16 July, they were taken to Münster again where the whole sixty were examined by military court, many of them individually, but the court got no satisfaction, for they all told the same story – that they were quite willing to do work of an agricultural nature, provided the hours and conditions were reasonable.

The next day saw the party entrained once more on a journey of some 15 kilometres only to a place named Kattenvenne, from which they walked along pleasant green lanes to the village of Vogelsang. It was like paradise to be there, Billson told us, after the smoke and grime of Dortmund. Work was of an agricultural nature, draining and fencing, levelling and clearing; they only worked for eight hours daily and were well treated. But poor old Billson had only enjoyed a week of this luxury, having been suddenly ordered back to Rennbahn on 24 July to be imprisoned ever since in a cell in Block II.

And now here he was amongst us again. The reason for his recall to Münster and for his imprisonment in Block II we could only guess, but it seemed probable that his share in the Dortmund strike was at the bottom of it. Anyway, why worry? Here he was, his troubles ended we hoped, and it was now up to us to celebrate his reunion.

Four of us had formed a 'Combine' in those days – Hicky, Webb, Hinks and myself; we shared all parcels we received and messed together from our common fund. Unfortunately, our old chum arrived on a day when the cupboard was bare, so that we had to postpone the celebration until the next day. Three or four good parcels turned up then, and Billson himself came in lucky too, for there were five for him that had been held up in the office pending his release, so that we had all that was needed for a real feast. There were French army biscuits, English bully beef, sardines, a large tin of pears, a tin of cream, sugar, butter jam and white bread – the latter tainted with mould, but not so badly that jam could not conceal this defect. We were as happy over the preparations that Thursday afternoon as children at a picnic. Eddie Hinks busied himself in the boiling of a large quantity of water on a fire he had made surreptitiously in the barrack-room stove. (I remember the excellent saucepan he had made for our 'combine' out of a large toffee tin; he had fitted it with a wooden handle and beaten its edges flat with a stone.) The rest of us joyously prepared the repast, hacking open the tins with a knife, spreading slices of bread with butter and jam, and laying everything out on a sheet of decent brown paper, enthusing over the magnificence of the array. Then there came a hissing and a spluttering from the stove, accompanied by a flow of rich Canadian curses, and followed by the refreshing aroma of hot tea. The preparations were complete. We gathered round, brandishing our 'Nestle's china' (our cups were usually empty milk tins), and dipped them into the steaming saucepan.

'A toast!' yelled Webb, raising his tin of tea. 'Let us drink the health of the strike leader and the eternal damnation of the sucking Huns!'

While we were in the act of drinking it, there came the sound of a heavy footfall at the far end of the room and the jarring thump of a grounded rifle.

'Billsohn! Billsohn! *Der Korporal* Billsohn *hier?*'

The excited falsetto of our podgy little *Feldwebel* grated across the harmony of our festivity and, turning our eyes apprehensively, we had a glimpse of an armed escort behind him. They stumped down the room towards us.

'*Der korporal ist hier! So! Jetzt müssen Sie nach Münster gehen, Billsohn! Weg! Loss!*' ('The corporal is here! Very well! You must set off for Münster at once, Billson! Be quick! Get a move on!').

We sat aghast. I could hear Billson swearing softly, but with great feeling. There was a moment's inactivity and then Hicky jumped up, his eyes blazing with an indignation that almost overawed the little *Feldwebel*. Hicky's knowledge of German was often useful, and his authoritative manner carried weight as he protested against the unreasonable request for immediate departure: the corporal was just going to have some food. He would be very quick over it. Could he have half an hour for food and packing up? Twenty minutes then?

The little German, his hands raised in horror, burst into a fury of ejaculation – the order said 'immediately!' – the guard was even now here waiting! *Veck*! *Los*! Billson!

Most men would have given in, but Hicky insisted: 'Why the hurry? The corporal cannot run away. All he wants is a few minutes to eat!'

All these moments were not wasted by the subject of the discussion: he was steadily getting inside as much of the good provender as he could stuff in between curses: and Hicky's persuasive powers proved to be of a high order, for the *Feldwebel* finally consented to allow ten more minutes for preparation as the escort stood by while we ate, leaning pensively on his rifle, marvelling at the sight of so much good solid food. We stretched the ten minutes into fifteen and then Billson disappeared again into the unknown. There was a trace of the old cheeriness on his face as he turned at the door, his hand raised in farewell. 'Cheerio chaps! I'll see you again some day!' But as we watched him go, our hearts were heavy. We knew neither where he was going nor why, and we felt that the road from Rennbahn to Münster might be the road to anywhere.

Before a week had elapsed we heard of him again. I was one of the usual hopeful crowd outside the parcels office, and I started as I heard my name called a few yards away. An Englishman was pushing his way towards me.

'Are you Tustin?' I nodded.

'I just came out of Münster clink this morning. There's a pal of yours in there, name of Billson, and he's sent you this.'

I took a grubby fragment of torn paper from the outstretched hand. 'What's he in quod now for?' I asked. 'How is he?'

'Don't know much about him. He's in solitary. Only seen him once or twice on exercise in the prison yard. Couldn't talk to him.'

I scanned the tattered paper, 'In solitary confinement waiting court martial for inciting men to mutiny at Dortmund. Get permission to bring me my parcels and a clean shirt. Billson.'

After discussing this very grave matter with my friends, we decided to ask our block *Feldwebel*'s advice. He was not an unfriendly soul. Of course we gave him no idea that we had received any letter – that would never have done – but we told him that we had heard rumours that the corporal was imprisoned at Münster on a very grave charge and asked him whether permission could be given for one of us to take some stuff to him. Hicky did the talking and again his persuasive powers won the day, the German promising to forward a letter I wrote requesting an interview with the *Kommandant*, Herr General von Steinecke.

Eventually, the general sent for me, and I was escorted through the main gate of the *Lager* to wait for some fifteen minutes outside the *Kommandantur* for the appearance of the great one. He came at last, a pompous old gentleman, stout and stiff, arrayed in beautiful blue uniform, his chest bearing a brave array of medals. My escort clicked his heels, called me to attention and saluted. The general saluted, bobbing his head as he did so in the curious manner affected by his kind. I stepped forward and saluted. The old man courteously saluted again. The punctilios thus duly observed, I put my request before him in English. His manner was gracious and encouraging as he strove to understand, but he evidently had only a very imperfect knowledge of English, for he choked and stuttered in his effort.

I enlarged on the necessity for providing Billson with clean clothing. '*Der Korporal ist louzzy? Was ist louzzy?*' I tried French. '*Ach! Sie sprechen Französisch! Gut!*'

We got on wonderfully well after that, and I found myself growing quite fond of the old boy, as he promised that he would issue an order for two Englishmen to be escorted every Saturday to Münster to take Billson's washing and parcels.

He beamed with benevolence as he made this promise, and I thanked him in all the languages I could lay my tongue to. I saluted. He saluted. The sentry saluted. We all saluted. And I was marched back to Block IV, wishing that every German had as kind a heart as our old *Kommandant*.

The next day being Saturday, Hicky and I blithely accosted our *Feldwebel* and demanded our escort. It was a rich experience to see two unwilling German soldiers turned out from the comfort of their beer and tobacco in their guard-room and given orders to take us to town. We watched them with interest as they sullenly loaded their old-fashioned rifles, and we noticed that the bullets were very thick and made of soft lead. We noticed too that they each loaded with a cartridge in the breech, and we reflected on the ease with which an accident might happen to us on the road. Their saw-edged bayonets were discomforting, as they made threatening gestures to indicate what would happen if we tried any tricks.

Although they were unpleasant people to have behind us, we enjoyed the sensation of trudging along a tree-bordered road once more and seeing the cornfields waving in the breeze.

Münster looked peaceful enough, its open-air cafés and beer gardens bathed in summer sunshine, and we thought what a pleasant day we might have together but for the sullen guards behind us. The civilians we met eyed us curiously but without hostility as we marched from the broad main street into narrow cobbled alleys towards the civil prison. We were conducted into a room, where two officers sat writing, and after a wait of some ten minutes, during which our presence was entirely disregarded, one of them gave an order. There was another long interval of waiting and then a door opened and in walked our old friend Billson.

Prison discipline be damned! – we sprang forward to greet him, oblivious of scowling guards and bespectacled officers – shook his hand and asked him how he was. In another moment we were hurled backwards, and amidst a fury of strafing I caught the words *'sprechen'* and *'verboten'*. One of the officers then took the opportunity of preaching a forceful sermon on what was apparently the virtue of silence, emphasising his points by banging the table with a revolver. I wished he would not be so emphatic, for the weapon pointed fairly consistently in my direction.

We emptied our bundles on the floor, and when we saw the minute care with which every article was examined, we felt glad that we had not attempted to secrete anything *'verboten'*. Clothing was shaken and the seams felt and scrutinised; loaves of bread, already cut in half by the censors at Rennbahn, were again probed and subdivided. A few books we had included in one parcel were set aside for closer scrutiny, and it was some days before Billson received them.

I think even the gaolers sensed the pathos of this meeting with our old friend, under conditions of silence and suspicion, and realised the utter isolation of this English corporal, a prisoner in prison, for they made no demur when we gripped hands once more before marching away.

It was some hours after our return to Rennbahn that I felt a scrap of tightly folded paper in one of my side pockets. What was my surprise, on pulling it out, to find it a letter from Billson, which he had evidently managed to slip in unobserved by anyone. It gave us very little information, only warning us to be ready to exchange missives whenever we went to see him and asking us to try to find out when his trial was to take place. We wondered as we read it whether he knew that the death penalty was a possibility, and we groaned at our helplessness. We could do nothing either directly or indirectly: there was no means of reporting his case to any neutral consul who would see fair play, and it was easy to imagine a German court passing the capital sentence. Anyway, the case was black against him. He had certainly advised the prisoners at Dortmund to cease work, and cessation of work might easily be interpreted as mutiny. The thought of our old comrade being led out some morning to die alone before a German firing party hung over us like a cloud. And all we could do for him was to make our weekly visits to the gaol and to slip cheery letters and bits of news into his fist as we shook hands.

All through the winter of 1915, Hicky and I made these journeys to Münster, and still there came no news as to the date of our friend's trial. We could see that the long confinement and suspense was telling on him. He became pale and thin, until we should scarcely have recognised him; and his letters sometimes gave signs that even his indomitable spirit was giving way under the strain of anxiety and utter loneliness. He told us afterwards that our visits were the only events he had to look forward to and that, but for our letters, he might have lost grip entirely.

It was surprising how easily we managed to exchange these secret messages. Only once did we bungle it – I had closed my hand upon the scrap of paper an instant too late, and the letter dropped under the very eyes of the four or five Germans around us. My boot was over it as soon as it touched the ground, but it seemed incredible that it had not been seen. Then, stooping to unfasten and fasten my boot-lace, I rose with the missive in my hand.

Our goings to and from the city were usually devoid of incident, but we nearly caused a great uproar in the street on one occasion by attempting to persuade our escort to allow us to have a drink of beer. We had a few marks in our pockets; the weather was hot; the escort, one guard only on this particular day, seemed a genial type, elderly and corpulent, and 'larded the earth' in true Falstaffian manner as he walked; the omen seemed propitious. We began to throw out hints.

'*Bier ist gut? Nicht?*' (Beer is good, isn't it?)

He nodded in hearty agreement – '*Jawohl!*' (Certainly!) '*Wir haben Durst!*' (We are thirsty!)

We waited, hoping for some sign of sympathy, but the worthy man, seeming dull of comprehension, plodded steadily onwards, mopping his beaded brow. I remember we were just passing a wooden statue, probably of Hindenburg, that had been set up in a square just off the main street: it was a huge figure, some thirty or forty feet high, with ladders against its sides, and it was in process of being studded with nails that people were allowed to hammer into it, on payment of a small sum of money per nail, the idea being, I suppose, to raise money to win the war. Hicky gave up hinting and explicitly suggested that the old soldier should lead us up some side street to a quiet little place round the corner for a drink of beer.

Comprehension suddenly burst upon the worthy man. He halted, his honest face wrinkled with emotion. We halted too.

Then the storm broke – such an excited spate of eloquent wrath that it seemed to fill the entire street. Passers-by stayed their steps to listen. Patriots up on the statue ceased their hammering to crane their necks towards us. A crowd of the good citizens of Münster formed about us in no time, while our guard standing astride with rifle grounded in front of him yelled to the wide world the story of our villainy. One or two of the crowd yelled in sympathy, and the atmosphere rapidly became hostile.

'All this about a glass of beer!' muttered Hicky. 'What a damn good thing we didn't ask for champagne!'

The situation was very unpleasant, and I could see one or two German officers striding towards the crowd. I had a sudden inspiration – if we moved on, the guard was bound to follow.

'Come on Hicky!' We strode forward where the press seemed thinnest. The guard followed, 'burbling as he came', and Hicky interpreted with a chuckle – he was going to report our wickedness to the *Feldwebel* as soon as ever we arrived. Whether he did so or not I don't know, but no disciplinary action was taken.

We made several attempts to get a drink when in Münster, but although we never again caused a social riot, we never got any beer.

Eventually, on 19 February 1916, Billson's trial took place and our weekly outings ceased.

The court consisted of six German officers, and an attempt was made to place the whole responsibility for the strike upon the corporal's shoulders, most of the strikers being summoned to give evidence.

For five or six hours the questioning went on, the witnesses being subjected to browbeating cross-examination.

One and all they perjured themselves and denied firmly every suggestion that the corporal had advised them to cease work.

In spite of the loyal attitude of his friends, it looked for a time as though things must go ill with Billson. The Court was anxious to find a scapegoat. When the case for the prosecution ended, prisoner and witnesses alike could not but fear the heaviest punishment for the corporal.

The fact that Billson's lawyer was a German did not increase the comfort of those among his friends who were more inclined to optimism.

Their uneasiness, however, was put to flight when the able German advocate had addressed the Court for five minutes. They listened to his forceful and impassioned appeal with renewed hope and growing respect. The Court was impressed; it was under the sway of a dominant personality, a gifted orator.

When the defence concluded and, verdict considered, judgment was finally pronounced, it brought relief and joy to all concerned in the alleged mutiny.

'Fourteen days *strenger Arrest*' (strict detention), for Billson and his companions alike; nothing more, thanks to the eloquence and skill of a German lawyer.

Chapter 7

Russians, Gurkhas, Moroccans

During the long months of Billson's imprisonment, our life in the *Lager* saw many changes, old hands continually departing into the unknown, and batches of new prisoners arriving. On the whole, more men must have come in than went away, for our quarters became more and more congested. Accommodation was doubled by replacing our single layer of straw mattresses by two tiers of hammocks; our discomfort was doubled too, for although cleaner than beds, these hammocks being made of coco-matting were so hard and rough and unyielding that if our bare hips rubbed on them during the night, we were red-raw in the morning; they were very cold too, for our blanket supply was totally inadequate.

If the atmosphere in our room had been bad before the introduction of hammocks, it was indescribably foul afterwards, the more so as a score of Russians were added to our number as well as forty or fifty French. The Russians in some cases carried fish heads and refuse in their pockets, some of them never washed, and they all had a deep-rooted objection to an open window. Although they were so big and so slow-moving and usually spoke in deep vibrant tones, there was something in their nature that always reminded me of little children. Their impulses were kindly and generous and, although prone to sudden bursts of anger in which they were capable of brutal actions, they were usually gentle and good-natured. Sometimes, I remember, some of them got drunk and then once or twice there was an ugly fight, in which men were seriously injured. I came across a victim of one of these drunken quarrels one day when I was looking round our block hospital. As I passed one bed, its occupant feebly beckoned me to his side and murmured '*Wasser! Wasser!*' (water). One hungry brown eye looked pleadingly from a mass of bandages about his head and face, and as I raised him to drink, I felt hard plaster about his ribs. I could not get the story of his injuries out of the man himself, for I was as ignorant of his language as he of mine, and I imagined that they must have been inflicted by the Germans in some dispute about work; but a French *infirmier* (hospital orderly) soon disabused my mind of that notion. It seems that in some brawl, one of his own NCOs had stabbed him in the chest with a knife, and then kicked him so viciously about the head and body as he lay on the ground that his jaw was fractured and a couple of ribs broken.

On one occasion during the winter, we had a little scrap with the Russians in our own room. Charlie Black, a quiet small-built man of the DLI (Durham Light Infantry), whose soul loathed stinks and dirt of every kind, obtained a wooden bedstead one day from somewhere or other and put it for himself right under the open window, falling asleep that night in a delicious draught of cold fresh air. He was aroused an hour or so later by a feeling of suffocation and found his window shut tight. He reopened it, only to have the same experience again; and after opening it a third time, he lay awake determined to wreak vengeance upon the man who tried to shut it. I knew nothing of what was going on until I was awakened by all the noises of a 'rough house', thuds and grunts mingled with a stifled yelling and snarling – and looking down from my top hammock, I could see in the light that filtered in from the arc lamps outside a kind of rugby scrum surging round Charlie's bed, a dozen hairy Russians with Charlie in their midst. When Coucher and one or two more of us had restored order, Charlie explained the origin of the uproar: he had caught one of the devils in the act of shutting his window, and when he had punched his nose, a dozen more of them had come to have theirs punched too.

A striking contrast to these big white men from the North were the little brown Gurkhas from the South, who came to Rennbahn in September 1915. They took to prison life very badly, becoming weary and listless, too 'fed up' even to kill the lice which swarmed upon them. I took a special interest in one youngster, Bhim Singh Thapa, who had been servant to his English officer and could speak a little English, and I remember how he demurred when I suggested he should wage a campaign against the vermin.

'Leave them to live!' he said simply. 'They too belong to God.' And then he recited in his gentle voice a short poem:

Turn, turn thy hasty foot aside,
Nor crush the helpless worm.

I listened with delight until he reached its end, but I stuck to my guns telling him that a British soldier's first duty was to keep himself clean, and soon we were busy with bloody thumbnails over his grimy shirt and trousers. Then I showed him how to deal with the eggs which abounded in the trouser seams, running a candle flame up and down them and making a jolly crackling. I rejoiced in this frizzling process, pointing out that lice and their eggs were evils which had to be destroyed. But Bhim Singh was not happy: to his contemplative mind all living things were God's creatures. I sometimes asked him how he could square this philosophy with the object of his journey westwards, the killing of Huns; but he could never explain that at all and would turn the subject, speaking in his quaint lilting English of the beauty of the hill country near his home in the Darjeeling district. He was consumed with a burning desire to see once more the snowy summits of the great mountains rising above the green plantations and forests of India. Poor lad! His wish was never realised, for a year after my return to England, I received this letter from Zossen, the camp to which all native colonial prisoners were removed from Rennbahn in November 1915.

Halbmond Lager,
Zossen, Germany.
20.9.17.
Many thanks for the nice photo which you sent, in the name of Bhim Sing who has been died by the illness, so I got it as he was my friend and countryman, so I am informing you that you should not be anxious for him in hearing his sad news.
from Yours sincerely,
4984 Bhawan Sing Pun.
2/8 Gurkha Rifles.'

I have often wondered what percentage of prisoners died in Germany and how many have succumbed to the effects of captivity since their return home. If statistics were obtainable, it is my opinion that the highest rate of mortality would be seen among either the Russian or the Gurkha prisoners in Germany. Not that the latter were ill-treated, but the climate killed some and several seemed to pine away from the sheer misery of imprisonment.

Before they left, there was an amusing fight between some of them and a number of French coloured troops.

I was watching a few Gurkhas kicking a football about in the block, when suddenly the ball struck a passing Moroccan violently on the back of his head. He was a peculiar looking fellow with voluminous sleeves and long sweeping garments, who might have stepped out of the pages of some wild desert romance, a curious blend of cruel ferocity and dignity, and I was amused to see him pick up the ball and run off with it in a great rage, the Gurkhas after him.

On the recapture of the ball, I noticed the offended warrior gather his comrades about him and indulge in a few minutes of impassioned oratory. Then there came a wild outcry and, dashing into the barrack rooms to seize any weapons they could find – pokers and shovels and brooms, but mainly brooms – the Arabs advanced in a savage rush that swept our little Indian friends pell-mell before them.

My pride conquered my alarm – I refused to give ground before the hordes of Islam – and I hoped to be accorded the privilege of a non-combatant observer. My prayer was granted; the rush swept by me. But a British sergeant who chanced to be walking harmlessly across to his room, utterly unaware of any trouble, was not so fortunate. Strolling round the corner of the canteen, he found himself unaccountably assailed by an infuriated Arab brandishing a broom and had only just time to duck and so escape the full force of the smashing blow aimed at his head. The broomstick struck his shoulder and snapped in two. Hurling the light and comparatively harmless length of stick left in his hand at the sergeant, the Arab darted forward to grab the heavy end from where it had fallen and again attacked his bewildered victim. The shortened broom swung backwards, mallet fashion, with deadly intent, but by this time I had reached the spot and was able to catch it from behind before it descended and to seize the man round the waist in an attempt to throw him. As I did so, I was myself seized from behind and in no time found myself on the ground with a couple of evil-smelling desert warriors on top of me and the knobby ends of what looked like hundreds of brooms whirling above my head. It was only the opportune arrival of the German guard upon the scene of conflict that saved me from destruction. My assailants fled before their bayonets, leaving me uninjured but filled with a most unchristian hatred for my Mohammedan brothers.

After the departure of the Gurkhas to Zossen, we settled down to the dreary winter, and the year 1915 dragged to its close without any changes in our circumstances and without any signs of the longed-for allied break-through. As Christmas approached, Anderson, our artist, set to work with a jelly pad, turning out a series of Christmas cards to be sold for the benefit of necessitous prisoners, but save for these and a welcome increase in the number of parcels, the festive season passed almost unnoticed.

On New Year's Eve I kept vigil with Hicky, defying discipline by sitting over the dying embers in our room stove until 1916 had begun. Scurries of rain and hail beat upon the roof and, as the wind blustered and bellowed outside, I remember how we thought of the men in the trenches that morning and how we contrasted their lot with our own. We realised that, so long as the flow of parcels continued, we were infinitely better off than they and that we had every chance of surviving the war and of enjoying the fruits of the final victory we could no longer help to win, and yet how gladly would both of us have exchanged our lot for life in the trenches.

My diary is practically a blank as far as the first month of the New Year is concerned, but, if my memory is correct, it was during January that a great fire occurred in a Münster munitions works. [The fire actually occurred on 21 December 1915.]

The first intimation we had that anything was wrong was a reverberating rumble like the beginning of a big thunderstorm, and then came a succession of crashes that brought us all out of our rooms agog with curiosity, hoping to see a squadron of allied aeroplanes dropping bombs near the *Lager*, but nothing was visible. The detonations continued at intervals during the afternoon and, as darkness began to fall, a great glare in the sky above the town enabled us to guess what the trouble was. We watched with joy as the glare became brighter and the concussions more violent; sometimes we could hear the crackling of small arms ammunition and occasionally heavy debris squealed and whined over our heads like great shells. For a long time we were content to stand, enjoying the sight and sound in silent rapture, but when our very barracks were shaken by one long succession of exceptionally severe explosions, some of our more excitable Gallic comrades were unable to suppress their delight, and the nerves of the sentries, already worn by anxiety and fretted by an occasional half-stifled British cheer, gave way entirely as there suddenly burst forth the triumphant rhythm of the Marseillaise. With shouts of rage the guards came at us with their bayonets and drove us to our rooms.

It must have been a serious disaster, for the explosions continued most of that night and there were sputterings and cracklings for a day or two afterwards. Billson, on his return to Rennbahn a few weeks later, told us that the noise in his prison had been deafening, and the consternation of the Germans there had amounted almost to a panic.

He described with glee how he had pulled himself up by the bars of his grilled window and hung there to see as much as possible until his arms were cramped. We never knew the cause of it all. Rumour of course was busy – an allied airman had dropped a lucky bomb, a Russian prisoner employed in the factory had struck a match – but I doubt whether the German authorities ever knew themselves.

Chapter 8

Brutalities

As time went on, those of us fortunate enough to consider ourselves as permanent residents at Rennbahn made ourselves more and more comfortable. Sometime during the winter, fate had flung Jack Harris into our block; he was a fat, jolly, little, middle-aged man, who had been on the stage as a comedian in happier days, and his services to the concert committee of the British Social Club made our theatrical entertainments more successful than ever. He managed to get a Pierrot troupe together. Eddie Hinks and a fellow named Fielder did the stage carpentry for them, Anderson the scene painting, and a Canadian named Deslie was stage manager.

Another development along quite different lines was a students' society. Some of us had formed a class to study the German language under M. Tyrol, a Frenchman who had been a teacher of languages in Edinburgh, and in the spring of 1916 we endeavoured, by working upon the respect for education which we knew existed among the Germans, to obtain official sanction for the formation of a whole series of classes. We achieved our main object. Permission was given for some fifty 'students' selected by the Committee of the Social Club, who wished to devote time to certain specific subjects, to move their belongings into Room 2 in Block IV. It was like ascending from the lowest hell to the highest heaven. Goodbye to our matting hammocks and to the lice and the sardine-like odour of dirty, densely-packed Russians. Room 2 was airy and light; it was furnished with the type of rough bedsteads for which we had envied the French sergeants; and it possessed one or two long trestle tables and benches. We could have been happy there if only we had not been prisoners.

I can't remember that we did much study. Our theatrical artistes studied their parts; some of us tried to learn French and German, and one enterprising lad had a shot at Russian, but I question very much whether the amount of work we did justified our existence as a students' society.

I imagine that the general's motives in allowing us so many privileges were, like most motives, mixed. He was a kindly old gentleman and was glad to behave chivalrously to the prisoners under his charge; but behind his gracious condescension must have been the feeling that it was a good thing to have a prison camp in Germany that could be used as a show place to impress any neutral ambassador who might take it into his head to enquire into the German treatment of prisoners of war.

Von Steinecke's character and the question of atrocities in general were the subjects of endless discussion among us. I can remember in particular one sunny afternoon in May, when a number of us were sitting on the sand at the edge of the Lagerstrasse, pursuing these topics with a zeal which at times amounted to heat. There was Anson, a Canadian recently returned from the coke ovens in some industrial town; Hicky was there too, and Charlie Black, the quiet 'student in arms' type of fellow who had fought the Russians in Room 9 in order to keep his window open; Charlie had had some experience of coke ovens too.

I had been suggesting that our captors were not as bad as they were painted, and as I spoke I could see Anson's choler rising.

'You can say what you like, Tustin; they are a bunch of fat, ugly bastards; if you ever meet a good one, kill him quick before he turns bad.'

I demurred at this sweeping generalisation: 'They are no worse than we would be in the same position. They don't feed us – but then, man! They cannot feed their own civilians properly: I bet thousands of their old folk and their children are dying for lack of good food. As for using prisoners to help run their mines and factories, what else can they do? With every available man in their army, they are using their own women folk as labourers. And when you fellows raise hell and say you won't work except on our own conditions, is it any wonder that you get a rifle butt in your ribs or a bayonet prick in the thigh? You know very well that they are putting up a damned good fight even though it is for a rotten cause.'

Anson's bloodshot eyes glared balefully. 'That's just the sort of tripe to expect from you suckers that have managed to wrangle staff jobs and have never been outside the shelter of this camp. You don't know the first thing about the bloody Germans. You get your parcels regular as clockwork. You have your theatre and your concerts. You want to get down a sucking mine and do some work. You don't know you're born!'

I looked at the haggard features of the Canadian, noticing his sallow skin and the nervous twitch of his hands. I felt unable to dispute his suggestion that I was immeasurably more fortunate than most prisoners, and I was relieved when Charlie Black took up the discussion.

'We don't want to say that the old square heads are paragons of loving virtue, old man! They're not, but are they much worse than we are ourselves? And are we in a position to see them clearly enough to judge them fairly? They have done some beastly things. But some of us chaps are just as bad. Fitz Simmons has a knife with notches on its haft to mark the tally of German wounded whose throats it has cut: he says he used to prowl about in No Man's Land at night searching for them: he may be a liar, of course, but somehow I think it's true. Then there's that wizened little Gurkha in Block IV with his bag of German ears. And did you hear Sergeant Addison's story of the fifty Saxon prisoners who 'disappeared' on their way back to our support lines? Their escort reported that they had lost them in a barrage. I'll bet many a thousand prisoners on both sides have been butchered in cold blood. Some of our chaps boast how they found a Hun buried to his shoulders in heavy debris as they were clearing up a bit of line we had captured. The poor devil was howling for help: they helped him all right; helped him clean out of all his misery with a few well placed bombs. The Froggies can tell some funny stories too. It's a bloody beastly war!'

'Who started it?' snarled Wallinger, a little Cockney. 'You want to read about what the swine did in Belgium!'

Black raised his eyebrows – 'I don't believe all the yarns that are knocking about. That crucified Canadian incident at Ypres, for instance, strikes me as the invention of some bright lad that wanted the Canooks to fight good and fierce and not be too kind-hearted.'

'But that sure happened!' broke in Anson. 'I knew a man who saw the poor guy taken down. A sergeant he was and still breathing when they got to him!'

Again Black's eyebrows expressed incredulity. 'It's all a question of evidence,' he said decisively. 'A fellow hears a sensational story that fits in with all the prejudices he has absorbed from a patriotic press. He repeats it in good faith as something he has heard. And then he begins to tell it as something he has himself seen. The lapse into the first person is easy; it increases the value of the yarn and makes it more impressive. But how the lies originate beats me.'

Anson's patience had evaporated entirely by the time Black had finished speaking, and he burst into a torrent of good Canadian. 'Aw! Shooks! Charlie! You're just telling a lot of b*** s***!'

For a moment I feared we were on the verge of a serious row, for the Canadian's nerves were on a hair trigger, and Charlie, despite his apparent gentleness, was liable to resort to very abrupt violence when provoked, as certain Russians in our block could testify.

It was Hicky who intervened. He jerked our minds right back from mythical crucifixions to the immediate present. 'What's happening at the gate?' he asked abruptly.

We watched as the sentries were drawing back the big bars, and three prisoners entered under the escort of two dusty guards. There was something unusual even for a prison *Lager* in the appearance of utter misery presented by this tiny party. Their gait had a peculiar stiffness; they looked abject and ill; and so nondescript were their ragged clothes that it was impossible for us to distinguish their nationality.

'Russkies?' queried Wallinger as they limped slowly by us down the Lagerstrasse. 'Russkies, hell!' The Canadian was on his feet staring white-faced as they trailed into the entrance of our block. 'It's Jock Lindsay and two other lads from "God's own country".'

We hurried after them to find that Anson was right. They were three Canadians who had left the *Lager* only a few months previously to go on *Kommando*, but we were so shocked by the change this short time had wrought in them that we could do nothing for the moment but grip their hands in silence. I have seen men dejected; I have seen men in hysteria, nerves shattered from shell shock, weeping in the agony of fear of death; but nothing has ever wrung my emotions as did the sight of these three broken prisoners of war. I had seen them leave the camp erect and light-hearted, striding into the unknown with that jauntiness of body and of mind so characteristic of the Canadian; and here they were, some six months later, reduced almost to the piteous level of the most wretched Russians.

'Have you any food to spare, boys?' they asked hoarsely. 'Guess we're all in.'

As luck had it, for once our combine had a full larder, so that in a few minutes we had a meal spread at one end of the trestle table – white bread, bully beef, butter, jam and a tin of fruit – we brought out all our treasures. But our guests were too exhausted to manifest the signs of pleasure we longed to see. They ate listlessly, without enthusiasm.

Other fellows in our room contributed tit bits, Anson bringing out a much-prized tin of maple syrup. 'Say! You guys will sure be jake here!' he shouted cheerily, as he thumped the tin down before them and slapped Lindsay with rough good nature on the shoulder.

We were startled to see him shrink away, his face wrinkled with pain – 'For God's sake Anson, have a care! Look here.' – He drew back the loose collar of his grey back and exposed a mass of bruises. Then, stooping awkwardly, he raised the bottom of his trouser, showing the back of his calf striped black and blue and yellow.

A murmur of horror went up from us all. 'What did it? Are you all like this?' 'Yep. Guess we got beat up some!'

We dragged the story from them bit by bit. Working conditions on their *Kommando* had been exceptionally harsh, men there having been literally worked to death. Food was as usual inadequate but, to make matters worse, for some reason very few parcels ever reached them. Our three friends had put their heads together, plotting, waiting interminable weeks for the longed for opportunity to escape from this hell. At last it came. In the face of desperate hazard they seized it and got clean away, only to be recaptured after three days of liberty. They were unanimous in praise of the kindness of the civil police who caught them. For a day or two they had been fed and housed in a spirit of magnanimity, which they had never previously dreamed of associating with the name of Germany, but then their troubles had begun. They were handed over to a military escort and taken back to the camp from which they had escaped. On arrival, they were locked in a cell and kept there for hours without food or drink till close upon midnight, when they were each taken in turn down a number of subterranean stone stairs into a large cellar full of German soldiers. There, by the orders of a *Feldwebel*, who owed them some special grudge, they were stripped entirely naked and thrashed with lengths of insulated cable into unconsciousness.

'When I was shoved in,' Lindsay said, 'I was dazzled by the lights, but there was a whole bunch of Huns sitting on benches round the walls, and through a haze of tobacco smoke I had a glimpse of old Harry being pulled on his back by the heels into a corner. I was just standing wondering if he was dead; and then some bastard jumped on me from behind, and I was spread out face down on the floor with a Hun at each arm and leg. I never had the chance of a fight for it.'

They had been given three days to recover from their beating before being brought back to Rennbahn to await trial for attempted escape.

We received this story in a silence broken only by the sound of muttered curses. What could we do? We felt completely hopeless.

Dear God! – is anyone so utterly helpless as a prisoner of war! If only we could pay the devils back!

I think it was the little Londoner who first broke silence and suggested a line of action. 'Old Steinecke's only a bloody Hun himself, but he won't stand for this. Let's ask for an interview with him.'

Then Hicky, ever resourceful, offered a line of action. 'Look here!' he cried. 'There's a French doctor in Block I hospital just now. I know him. He's a good chap. Let's see him first. Come on up to Block I!'

But the three Canadians, unwilling to stir their stiffened limbs, raised feeble objections – 'What's the use of seeing doctors anyway? All we want to do is to lie down and to keep on lying down. Even if the doctor sent him any report, do you think your sucking old general would do anything but laugh?'

It did not take us long to overcome this attitude, for the poor chaps were in a state of apathy in which they could not maintain a lengthy resistance. The ensuing medical inspection revealed a sight more dreadful than anything we had imagined. From head to foot they were one gigantic bruise, not a patch of white skin visible upon their backs, and even on the front of their bodies, weals marked where the rubbered wire had whipped round ribs and thighs. Here and there the skin was broken, showing the raw flesh beneath it.

I have never seen a man more distressed than was the little French doctor. He danced around them as though possessed. '*Sacre nom d'un nom, d'un nom! Je vais ecrire une lettre. Le general verra lui meme ces pauvres gars! Il faut qu'il vienne tout de suite, tout de suite!*' ('Sacred Name! I shall write a letter! The general himself shall see these poor lads! He must come at once!')

He wrote his letter. We waited. Half an hour passed by and then there arrived on the scene a German army doctor. The Herr General was engaged; he could not come. The two doctors were to examine the cases together and submit to von Steinecke their joint report.

We observers were cleared out of the hospital at this point of the proceedings, but as we went we had time to notice that the German's indignation was almost as fervent as that of his French colleague had been; and their report must have been a strong one, for we heard long afterwards that the *Feldwebel* responsible for the beating had been degraded and sent to the Russian front, together with some of his assistants. We hoped that they were destined to perish there.

A crowd of some thousand newly arrived prisoners at Rennbahn camp, 1916.

The arrival of the camp commander, General Herr von Steinecke.

The general and his aide-de-camp passing the sentry guards at one of the entrances: 'General Herr von Steinecke was a portly, white-moustached old gentleman, who obviously bore us no special ill will and who was especially kind to the French.'

Outside the parcels office, New Year's Day, 1916: the carts were pulled by the prisoners, 'yoked like horses', from Hiltrup station, a few miles away: 'Were it not for these food parcels, sent from England and France, many prisoners would have died of hunger.'

Interior of Rennbahn church with the English and French pastors. The English pastor (seated) arranged concerts, the profits of which paid for the wood to make the church furniture. The organ was hired from the Germans.

French Symphony Orchestra: 'It was at Rennbahn that I heard my first symphony concert.'

The author (standing, 5th from the left) at Rennbahn with a group of French members of the *Caisse de Secours*: 'The *Caisse de Secours* was a ''Helping Fund'' originated by the French for the relief of necessitous prisoners of all nationalities.'

A scene from *Mon bébé*, an 'especially memorable' production by the French, in which all roles, male and female were enacted by men. Only a small number of prisoners, however, enjoyed these entertainments: 'There were only 6,000 men in the camp who could enjoy these privileges, while, outside it, wearing away flesh and bone in mines and munition factories, or scorching and suffocating among the heated fumes of coke ovens, were over 40,000 fellows who had been sent out from the camp ''on *Kommando*''. These workers are the men to write articles on German prison-life. They have no concerts, no libraries, no orchestras, nor have they energy to spare for football. Their lives are indescribably hard' (from 'Out of the Hands of the Hun' by H.W. Tustin, published in *The Bede*, the magazine of his old college at Durham, in December 1916).

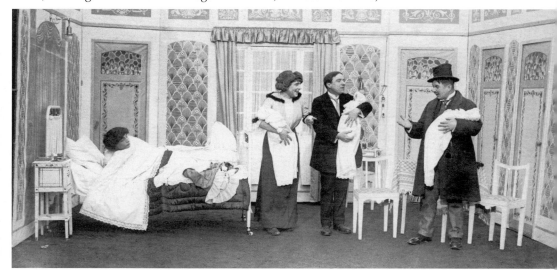

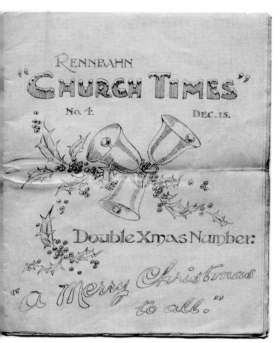

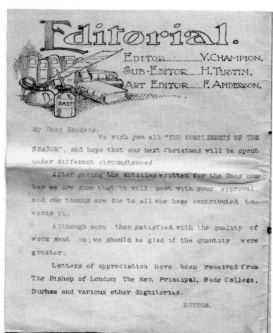

EDITOR............V. CHAMPION.
SUB-EDITOR.....H. TUSTIN.
ART EDITOR.....F. ANDERSON.

The *Rennbahn Church Times*, No. 4., December 1915: 'The *Rennbahn Church Times* made its appearance on 22 September [1915], with the drummer as its editor and myself as his sub. What a job we had in turning out a hundred copies of this every month!'

Christmas card, 1915, printed at Rennbahn: 'As Christmas approached, Anderson, our artist, set to work with a jelly pad, turning out a series of Christmas cards to be sold for the benefit of necessitous prisoners, ...'

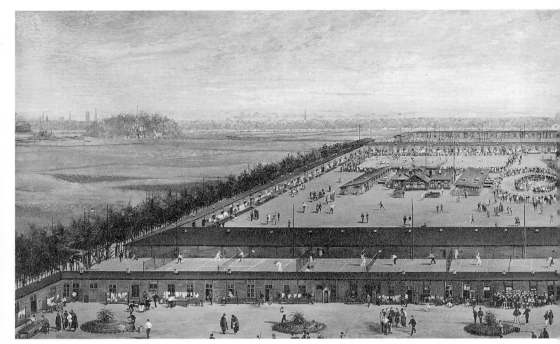

Rennbahn camp (1917). Auguste Potage, a French prisoner at Rennbahn, was ordered by the German authorities to produce this painting. It angered many prisoners, who saw it as German propaganda:

'Among the party was an outstanding person, a French artist, and he was ordered to paint a picture of the Rennbahn camp, Münster, which was to be presented to the Münster authorities for their public gallery. In the picture, he was to use his imagination and show all the possible activities and visual conditions of a German prisoner-of-war camp – a German *Kriegsgefangenenlager*. The canvas was a very large one and extraordinarily interesting, its real use being to influence coming generations of German 'humanity', which they knew would never be proclaimed by any that experienced it.

The general first impression one got was the overall size. It appears larger than it was. It shows much of what I have already described – football, boxing, French bands (never seen in the open). The round flower beds of flowers and shrubs. The triangular portion of lawn grass. These did not exist. The one thing I and many others longed for was to see even a blade of grass growing, or the sight of a tree. The artist certainly used his imagination. Look, a bowling green to the right of the picture – tennis to the left, and three courts at that. The picture gives that sense of freedom which is all so false and pictorial lying. It was the biggest job in the world to find an excuse to get out of the block for any purpose whatever. The many people on the dividing roadways may be true as it depicts the arrival of working parties pulling farm trucks or parcels etc., and possibly a parcel distribution. I can only sincerely hope that lovers of pictures will not be deceived if they ever see this picture, and get a false idea of what the German prisoner-of-war life was like.'

(from the memoir of Sgt Horace Reed, PoW at Rennbahn. *Imperial War Museum*)

Working prisoners did not receive their pay in official German currency but in prison *Lagergeld* (camp money). This was to prevent them accumulating large sums of money, which could have been used to bribe guards to help them escape and then pay their way through enemy territory to freedom. As with other camps, Rennbahn (also called 'Münster II') used its own specially produced currency; the coin shown here was used in the camp.

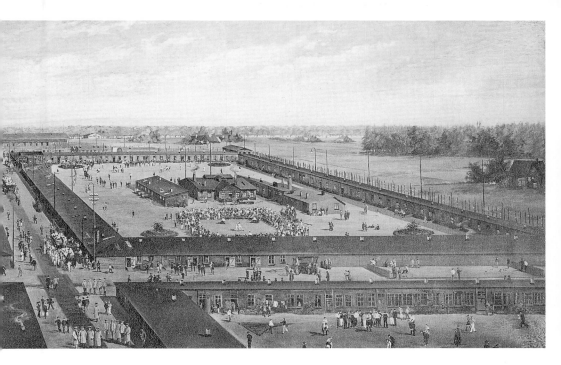

A view of Block I: the huts in the centre are the wash-houses and kitchen. The trees in the distance could not be seen by the prisoners, for no windows opened onto the outside.

A German lesson (author: middle row, third from the right): 'Some of us had formed a class to study the German language under M. Tyrol, a Frenchman, who had been a teacher of languages in Edinburgh.'

'Coucher' (real name Albert Croucher), the author's sparring partner: 'We had among us several good regimental boxers and, best of all, a champion middle-weight named Coucher, who had at one time been one of Carpentier's sparring partners and who could make rings round any other exponent of the noble art in the camp. In appearance the very personification of ruthless power, this professional fighter was really the soul of gentle good nature, encouraging even the most timid youngsters to spar with him and putting all his knowledge of boxing at our service. He has probably quite forgotten me, but I shall never forget him, nor the lessons I enjoyed from him. Above all, I remember the occasion on which I almost knocked him out, and the hiding he gave me afterwards.'

Gerrie Burk: following his escape, Burk had his passport photo taken in Rotterdam. The author listed this as one of the pictures to use in illustrating his memoir. Sadly, this photo was lost, but Burk's family and his old college (St Andrew's in Aurora, Canada) were fortunately able to provide these alternative photos to enhance this book.

Photo (1914/15) from the archive of St Andrew's College in Aurora, Canada.

Photo (1914/15) kindly provided by Valerie Beevor, Burk's granddaughter.

Post-war photo (mid-1930s) kindly provided by Peter Pilgrim, Burk's great nephew.

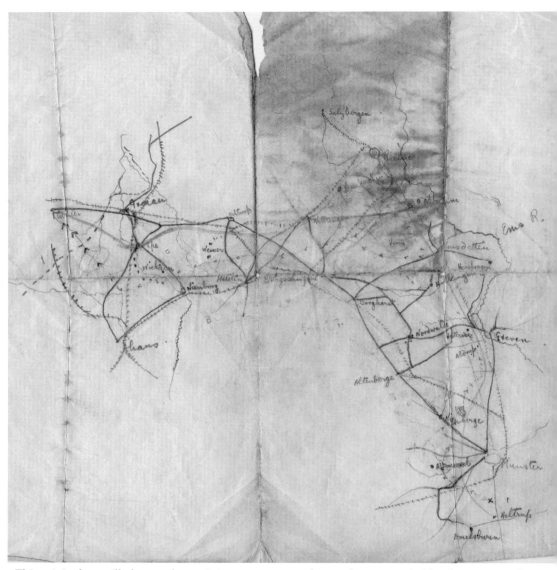

This original pencilled map, drawn in camp, was one of several maps carried by the escapees. It shows a longer, more circuitous route than the one actually taken (see next page) and was devised, presumably, to avoid human settlements and so reduce the risk of being seen. According to this memoir, however, the intended route was 'one which kept in view, at a distance, the main railway line leading to Holland', which would have led them more directly to Enschede via Burgsteinfurt. They evidently set out along this route, but due to the many farms, barking dogs and tiny fields (which inevitably meant more hedges to negotiate and slow their progress), decided it was 'madness to court disaster by any further progress so near to the line'.

It is remarkable that this map, drawn in pencil on thin, poor-quality paper, survived the arduous journey, considering that it was carried by Tustin as he swam across a flooded river, slept in damp ditches and evaded the shots of frontier guards. It is yet more remarkable that the map is still in existence, a century after its creation.

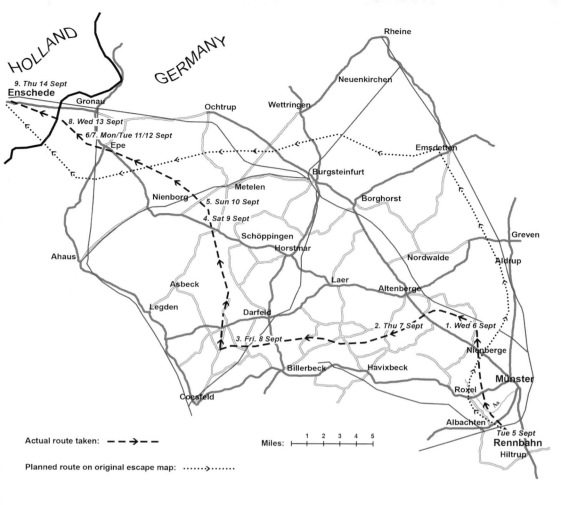

Actual route taken: – – –>– – –

Planned route on original escape map: ·······>·······

Miles: |—1—2—3—4—5—|

Following his escape, Tustin drew a map of the actual route taken, which has unfortunately been lost. However, among Tustin's effects was discovered an old 1916 war-office map of the Münster area. Pencil marks, drawn by Tustin, indicate the course that was followed (see right). Using this map and the clues within the memoir, the lost map has been recreated (see above). The escapees took nine days to reach Holland. They often strayed off course and 'lost hours in fruitless wanderings', so this map is approximate rather than exact, especially with respect to their daily progress.

ember 1916 *going rude NW*

SEPTEMBER 1916

SUNDAY 10
12th after Trinity

In little wood
by Orchard moss + pine branches
Bull broke loose.

Very tired Travelled in circles
night NW.
about No apples.
in ditch on moors — furze moor
— stayed there all night
Damn the moon.
ate bully beef.

MONDAY 11

TUESDAY 12
No travelling
In a ditch on moors
Rations finished — no
more orchards
Expected crossing frontier
to night road River
Many hours

WEDNESDAY 13
Going heavy. road + bog
In a barn on moors
— a dog nearly does us in
Bells + dogs. Misery
Cold + hunger
Turnips carrots + potatoes

THURSDAY 14
Shot at. Ram. moon.
Over + into Enschede
Kindly Dutch. Morning in
klink. Afternoon 1.50 train
for Rotterdam

FRIDAY 15
Rigged up — new outfit
Afternoon + evening in
town — Ham + egg tea + g
Musical evening — LDT.

SATURDAY 16
Scevening + the Hague
Peace Palace. De Wendt
burnab death place.
Left Rotterdam on
Grenadier for Newcastle
Sea Sick. Left well
Memo.

Excerpt from the author's 'escape' diary, 10–16 September: Thursday 14: 'Shot at, …'

6   DE TELEGRAAF van DONDERDAG 14 SEPT.

A portion of the Dutch newspaper *De Telegraaf* found by the escapees, the first real sign that they had crossed the border into Holland: 'Something fluttered towards us on the road. It looked like a piece of newspaper. I stooped and picked it up … and trudged ahead still clutching my piece of Dutch newspaper like a precious talisman.'

Enschede, the Dutch frontier town that signalled freedom for the two escapees: 'It seemed very quiet and peaceful as we tramped along its cobbled streets, to the great interest of a few early risers, who stared at us curiously.'

Following their arrival in Holland, the escapees were escorted to Enschede police station: 'We were evidently expected to answer a fire of questions put to us in Dutch. As we could make no reply in the same language, we were shown into a small empty room. The door clanged to behind us, a bolt shot home, and we realised that once more we were prisoners. Too tired to be much perturbed, we ... promptly fell asleep.' When they awoke the escapees were treated with the utmost kindness, interviewed by an officer fluent in English, and later sent under escort, aboard the 1.50pm train, to Rotterdam.

The prisoner-of-war cemetery in Münster, with its war memorial: 'Prisoners bought the stone, and French masons sculptured it. . . . The graves were carefully tended by the prisoners.'

The author with members of his family outside the family home in Ponteland in 1917. Left to right: brother Arnold, mother Eleanor, Herbert (the author), brother Tom. (Eleanor's identity cannot be verified as no other photos of her are known to exist. Arnold's identity is also unconfirmed.)

Reunited sweethearts Herbert and Sybil. The photo was probably taken on the same occasion in 1917 as the family photo on the previous page and just before Tustin's posting to South Africa, as he is shown wearing the officer's uniform of a Second Lieutenant of the Royal Garrison Artillery.

The author as a cadet in February 1917: after his escape, Tustin received a commission and was posted to garrison duty in South Africa, where he served out the rest of the war.

Herbert and Sybil's wedding day on 3 August 1921.

Herbert Tustin with wife Sybil, daughter Lynette and son Graham, in Teesdale, *c*.1936.

Chapter 9

Humours of Prison Life

Memories of Rennbahn are not all vile. From the sombre monotony of that futile prison existence there stand out in my memory close friendships, flashes of humour and merry laughter.

Much of the humour that brightened our lives centred about linguistic difficulties – the attempts of English, French, Russians and Germans to make themselves mutually understood being often ludicrous in the extreme.

I remember one elderly Frenchman whose serious efforts to learn our English tongue provided mirth in plenty. He had been a portly citizen of Maubeuge in civil life and, despite his red and blue uniform, he still looked a civilian, a very harmless and avuncular civilian at that. His roomy nether garments alone were enough to cause laughter; they always suggested to me an exercise in some old-fashioned French primer – '*As tu vu les longs bons pantalons de mon oncle?*' or something like that.

It was in the summer of 1915 that I first noticed him. He was standing a few yards from our barrack-room door, benevolently regarding the attempts that Anson and I happened to be making to air our bedding. We had turned it all out on to the square in the hope that the sunshine might kill a few lice and generally sweeten things up.

'Let's give them a good shaking before we take them back,' I suggested, grabbing one of the cottony blankets by two corners.

Anson caught the other end. Flap! Out flew a cloud of dust and debris. Rejoicing in well doing and forgetful of the flimsy nature of these old and rotten bed coverings, we went at the job with more energy than wisdom. Suddenly, without any warning whatever, there came a terrific ripping sound and the fabric parted completely, leaving us each with a tattered half in his hands.

The silence in which we contemplated this catastrophe was broken by a thin and quavering falsetto. It was the voice of the citizen of Mauberge. 'Aaah Messieurs! You 'ave ze blanket cracked, ees eet not!'

For a moment we glared at him malevolently, but as we took in the comical aspect of this tactless gentleman, anger gave place to mirth and my companion burst into a roar of laughter. 'Guess you've said it, boy!' he shouted. 'This b****** is sure busted some!' and then we bundled the bedding into our quarters, making evil puns about cracked Frenchmen and cracked blankets in great good humour.

After this I often noticed the man. He used to wander about looking for opportunities of practising English and of airing his knowledge; he would sidle up to any group of British prisoners which appeared to him as reasonably docile, and then break in upon their conversation by declaiming with shrill pertinacity – 'Ze skai! Be'old eem! Eet ees blew, *n'est ce pas*? You say, eet ees blew. 'Ow say you?'

Generally the group would disperse muttering imprecations. Occasionally, undue pertinacity was rewarded by a well-placed kick into the midst of those roomy 'pantaloons'. But sometimes the poor man would find an Englishman willing to talk to him and to give instruction – and then, what language he learned! I was once attracted by the noisy mirth of an animated group of Tommies sitting in a corner of our block, and on approaching them, I found to my surprise that old 'Sky is blue', as we called him, occupied a place of honour in its midst.

'"Bloudy good", you say,' I heard the thin treble raised querulously. 'What is "bloudy"?' An expression of bewildered surprise spread over the Frenchman's face at the roar of laughter which greeted his query.

A little Londoner, Timson, who was obviously acting as temporary English instructor, shook his fist at the onlookers. 'Nix larfin, yer silly b*****s!' he threatened. 'Ow in 'ell can a chap give this poor b*****d a lesson with you all making a muckin' row like that?' And then he went on to explain the manifold abuses of the most abused word in our tongue.

'Say arfter me,' said the instructor, 'bloody nice day.'

The falsetto obliged. 'Zat ees good English, zen?' 'Bloody good English. Now say ...'

And so the lesson continued, the pupil's ludicrous expression of guileless trust as he mouthed words unprintable was too much for me, and I passed on, marvelling as much at the primitiveness of the teacher's humour as at the simplicity of his pupil.

I was on my way at the time to see Ducros, a Parisian with whom I read and conversed daily in French and in English with the idea of mutual benefit, and I told him how his compatriot's leg was being pulled, suggesting that he might throw out a few warning hints.

Ducros laughed, 'The silly fellow has what you call the deserts.' And then he told me of a German *Feldwebel* who was undergoing similar treatment by a group of Frenchmen whom he had to escort to Münster, three or four times weekly, on parcels fatigue: he was learning the most vile 'argot' under the impression that it was the language of the most cultured French circles.

This *Feldwebel* was a particularly offensive and pompous little beast. His principle method of learning French was to strut about indicating various objects in turn and authoritatively demanding their French names, which he solemnly entered up in a huge notebook carried for the purpose. He had been doing this in the goods yard at Münster station a day or two previously and had pointed to one of a number of casement window frames lying there awaiting removal.

Now the French word for this type of frame, as any schoolboy knows, is *'vasistas'*, and even more generally understood is the German phrase, *'Was ist das?'* ('What is this') pronounced in almost exactly the same way.

'Und was ist das?' asked the *Feldwebel*, touching the frame with a podgy forefinger. *'Un vasistas, Monsieur'*. For once at any rate the French corporal spoke truly.

'Ja! Ja! Was ist das denn!' The throatiness of the German's voice suggested irritation. *'Un vasistas, Herr Feldwebel!'* murmured the Frenchman sweetly.

'Jawohl! Ja! Ja! Ja! Und was ist das?'

Now the German was striking the wooden frame with his fist, his face empurpled with anger.

'Un vasistas!' mimicked the corporal, enjoying the joke.

The exhibition of Germanic fury that ensued, the 'Himmeling', and the 'Schweinering' – all was in vain; the Frenchman refused to do more than echo *'un vasistas'* until the *Feldwebel* retired, incoherent with wrath.

Ducros told me of this little episode in great style, with a wealth of gesture and an intensity of delight that made my heart warm to him. I had known him for many months and had had ample evidence of his common sense and general *savoir faire*. It happened at this time that I had a great trouble on my mind, a most awkward situation having arisen between myself and one of his countrymen, and I suddenly decided to take him into my confidence and ask for advice.

M. Tyrol, the teacher of languages, who was zealously trying to instil a little German into some of us, had asked me many months previously whether I would mind receiving a parcel of tobacco for him from his wife in Scotland.

'You see,' he had explained, 'I love ze English tabac. Zis German stuff is – what you call it? – muck, and our French supply is so poor also. But we *poilus* (Fr. French infantrymen) may not receive tabac from England. It is, 'ow call you it? – "in bond".'

I had promised lightly that any package of tobacco I received from Mme Tyrol should be duly handed over to him. And then I forgot all about it.

Later on I became a member of the committee of the *Caisse de Secours*. The weeks and months rolled on. Odd parcels of all kinds came to me for distribution among necessitous prisoners. And then one day I received a heavy and compact package, which proved to contain cigarettes and tobacco of really good quality, all in perfect condition.

Hicky and Coucher were with me as I unpacked this stuff, and I remember how the three of us glowed with pleasure as we sniffed at it.

'I am afraid this is for the Helping Committee,' I murmured regretfully; for, save that it had been ordered from and despatched by an Edinburgh firm, there was no clue as to the donor. I waited a few days in the expectation of a letter which might give instructions as to the disposal of its contents. But since none came and since I felt that these English smokes would be largely wasted if bestowed upon indigent French and Russians, I finally decided to dish them out as a gift from heaven to all the English in my block. And never was a gift more appreciated. The smoke of its burning brought an atmosphere of peace and good-will in which we one and all blessed the unknown giver. In a few days all that remained of the tobacco was a happy recollection.

Then, one bright afternoon, Tyrol bumped into me in Lagerstrasse. He was smiling cheerfully, and, after a handshake in the ceremonious French style, I remarked on the delightful sunshine. There was no cloud in the sky.

But Tyrol's spiritual contentment had nothing to do with the weather. He had something still better to talk of. 'My wife, she 'ave wrote,' he proudly announced. 'I 'ave two letters today.'

For the moment I was at a loss, wondering in a dazed fashion whether his obvious pride and joy had something to do with twins or triplets. Noncommittal interest seemed the wisest attitude – 'Good news?' I asked politely.

'Ze news most excellent!' he yelled joyously. 'She say she have sent ze tabac.'

And then suddenly I remembered. Tabac! My God! Here was the missing clue.

As through the roar of rushing waters, I heard the poor man's cheerful voice. 'You will observe for it at ze distribution of ze packets! You will remembair?'

I shook hands murmuring that I would never forget and passed on. Forget it! How I wished it were possible to forget. The sunshine was no longer beautiful for me. The murmur of the voices about me seemed to chant in minor cadence – 'She say she "ave sent ze tabac!" Poor Tyrol! He was a good sort. What could I do?

I had managed to keep out of his way ever since that meeting in Lagerstrasse, avoiding his German class and turning a corner whenever I caught a glimpse of him on the horizon; but his tobacco was ever with me, a load on my mind that never lifted.

This was the sad story I unburdened to Ducros. But, instead of manifesting the concern I had anticipated, he howled with delight.

'O! La! La! La! La!' he cried, tears of mirth dimming his eyes. '*La perfide Albion*! *Vous l'avez parfaitement voél*!' ('Oh treacherous England! You have thoroughly swindled him.')

'But what can I do?' I asked dolefully.

Ducros doubled himself up with laughter. 'Do? You must go to him! You must say, "Oh, dear M. Tyrol, I have given away all your so beautiful tabac!" He is so greedy a man also. He will have, what you call it? Ze bile!'

'Look here!' I had an idea. 'You know Tyrol. You see him for me and break it to him as gently as you can!'

'Ah, no, Monsieur!' Ducros became more serious immediately. 'He has ze choleric temperament, zis good Tyrol! He would say zings about you zat I your friend would not wish to hear.' And then there came another peal of laughter.

I left him still chuckling. It was some days before I finally decided to get my load of guilt from my chest. And then, when I entered Tyrol's room, my resolution paled before the glowing hopefulness of his enquiries. It seemed so much more merciful to allow this hope of his to die gradually than to kill it with one swift stabbing sentence. He offered me a cigarette – I noticed it was one of the despised 'petit caporal' brand – I declined it – I fled.

And as I write, I wonder whether M. Tyrol remembers that lost tabac as vividly as I do. My French acquaintances were not limited to the members of the *Caisse de Secours* and their circle of wealthy adjutants.

A knack I have of being able to read at sight almost any pianoforte or organ music brought me into close touch with the theatre and orchestral groups, and later on, in the summer of 1916, with a community of French protestants. I had played the organ several times to help Campon with his C. of E. Services, and occasional concert work as assistant accompanist had made me a little conspicuous among the more permanent residents of Rennbahn.

I was surprised, nonetheless, to find myself accosted one Sunday morning by a bearded little *infirmier*, who introduced himself as M. Manen, the French protestant pastor of the camp. None of his congregation was musical, he assured me.

Would I play the organ for their service on Sunday afternoons?

I thought of the wheezy harmonium thing, euphemistically referred to as the organ, and I groaned inwardly. I had just been churning out hymns on it for the English that very morning and felt that I had acquired enough virtue for the day without breathing an atmosphere of French sanctity most of the afternoon. Was this a justifiable occupation for a man who had spent his childhood slaving away at Czerny's *'Exercices de vélocité pour piano'*?

The good pastor felt my hesitation, for he redoubled his pleading, and when I consented, he almost fell on my neck in his gratitude, urging me to come and have tea with him after the service. Again I hesitated. My memories of teas with Frenchmen were not by any means thrilling, so far as the menu was concerned – and it was the menu that mattered most at Rennbahn – but I could think of no decent excuse and for politeness' sake accepted the invitation.

Never was politeness more sumptuously rewarded. I found my host had a room of his own, roughly furnished with bed and table and chairs, but as I entered, it was the table that held my gaze. Spread with a clean linen cloth, with places laid for two – cups, saucers, glasses, knives and forks and spoons – it presented a picture of such delight to a hungry prisoner as cannot be imagined.

The pastor beamed his pleasure at receiving me, and with my eyes on the table, I murmured the conventional French cliché that I was enchanted to visit him, feeling that I was indeed speaking the truth from my heart, for a scent of cooking, spiced with the suggestion of onion, stole deliciously to my nostrils; and a harmonious sound of cheerful stirring and a sizzling came from the end of the room, where a stoutly built rosy-faced man was busy over a saucepan.

As the pastor introduced this culinary artist as his orderly, I felt inclined to tell him that he could make music far better than any of mine. Then without more ado we sat down to the best meal I ever had in Germany.

The weird assortment and profusion of the victuals reminded me of college teas of happier days. Never was organist more generously paid. The hors d'oeuvre was sardines on toast and we washed them down with crème de menthe.

Rusks, bread spread with *paté de foie gras*, and biscuits smeared with jam and margarine were followed by the *pièce de résistance*: tinned rabbit and beans, served hot with roast potatoes. We drank beer with this – only German canteen lager, but it was beer. Then came an interlude during which we toyed with more rusks and jam and currant cake and cheese, while M. Manen and his orderly entertained me with the latest camp canards (rumours, wild news).

There were two sensational rumours that had provided an endless topic of conversation for a month or more. On 3 June all the flags over the *Kommandantur* had flaunted gaily, and we had been told by our *Feldwebel* that they celebrated the sinking of the English fleet in the German Ocean. Three days later, on 6 June, a persistent rumour spread abroad that Earl Kitchener was dead. Our *Feldwebel*, a good-natured little man, treated these reports very seriously. He was gaily emphatic as to the truth of the first, but even he seemed to doubt the second and to put it down either to some deep-laid English scheme for deluding the German command or to the desire of the German press to give good news to its readers. Most of us British prisoners, however uneasy we felt about them in secret, professed utter disbelief in both these reports, and I remember how I laughed at my host's concern about '*le* Lord Keetchenairrr'. It was easy to laugh as the feast was crowned by a glorious dish of tinned cherries liberally covered in preserved cream.

Then café noir was handed to us by the devoted Labeste and, as I puffed contently at one of my host's cigars, I expressed my warm appreciation of his extraordinary hospitality and enquired, as delicately as my limited knowledge of his language would permit, how he had managed to produce such a spread.

I gathered from his reply that his own food reserves had been supplemented by free-will offerings, contributed from their parcels by some members of his flock who desired to do honour to their new organist.

'But the potatoes, the onions?' I asked – 'They never came in parcels?'

'*Ah non, Monsieur!*' M. Manen smiled. 'It is '*ce bon Labeste!*' – with a deprecating wave of his hand, he indicated the cheery orderly – 'who sometimes goes on *corvée* (labour) to a nearby farm, who has large pockets – '*des poches extraordinaires*' – useful for carrying home any stray vegetables.'

Bantering the pastor for encouraging his servant to break the eighth commandment, I feigned horror at having been waited on by a thief, at the table of a minister of religion, too! 'What can be more virtuous in a French soldier than plundering the Germans?' smiled my host.

There came a roar of rage from Labeste – the word '*Allemands*' acted on him like a finger pressure on the trigger acts on a gun – '*Les Bosches!*' he snarled, his face no longer cheery, '*ces sont tous des voleurs! Les scelerats! Les animaux! Les especes le ****!*'

It was some time before M. Manen was able to calm him down, and then I remember how the talk turned upon our captors and their little ways. We discussed the madness of a new German colonel who had recently been visited upon us as a kind of assistant to the Herr General von Steinecke. I forget the man's name. He was kindly enough but quite mad. As there was nothing useful for him to do in the camp, he had made a new job for himself, acting as a kind of barber's tout. He made it the sole object of his life to see that every English prisoner had his hair cropped to the regulation German length – and this meant that we had to have our scalps, practically speaking, clean shaved. He used to wander foolishly about the camp searching for suitable victims. Having found one, he would gently but firmly remove his hat, grunting with satisfaction if he found much hair beneath it and adjuring the poor wretch in a curious mixture of French and German – he had no English – to '*hier kommen, coupez des chevoo*', and then he would lead him to the barber's shop and personally superintend the removal of the offending locks.

M. Manen, like most of his compatriots, was greatly amused at this treatment of English prisoners, for Frenchmen were not molested. He leaned over the table towards me, his cigar glowing in the gathering shadows of the room. 'Can it be,' he bantered, 'that the good colonel fears lest the English shelter little animals – *petits animaux* – in their hair?'

We laughed together at this shocking idea, and then the pastor asked whether there was any truth in the report that the mad colonel, dissatisfied with the work of the French barber, was actually handling the scissors himself.

As it happened, I knew all about this, and my host roared with delight when I told it.

My friend Hicky, the librarian, had a magnificent shock of fair curls of which in secret he was inordinately proud and which, thanks to the comparatively mild discipline of a college company, he had been allowed to retain. By bad luck he had one day left his library, just as the colonel was on the prowl, and had almost run into him as he rounded the entrance from Lagerstrasse to Block IV. Saluting decorously, he would have passed on blithely had not the German planted himself firmly in the middle of the entrance, rotund, immovable.

'*Monsieur! Der chevool! Sie haben der chevoo zu longs! Permettez-moi.*' His fingers caressed the nape of Hicky's neck, pulling playfully at the offending curls, and finally sweeping off his hat to reveal all their golden glory.

'And then the old b****** hooked me by the arm and marched me off to the sucking barber's, clucking like a damned old hen with a new chicken,' Hicky had told me indignantly.

The colonel, having seen him safely ensconced in the tonsorial chair with a towel round his neck, had fixed himself at the door looking triumphantly around the block for some new victim.

'As soon as I saw the old b******'s hindquarters,' said Hicky, 'I buzzed off out through the open window, towel and all.'

The furious amazement of the colonel, when, on looking round to see how the lamb was enduring the shearing, he found nothing but an empty chair, was described to me later on by the barber. For a long time he had stuttered and stormed incoherently, and then, suddenly struck by a bright idea, he had purchased on the spot a little clipping machine, which he ever afterwards carried in his pocket, insuring himself against any future trickery by clipping with his own hands a furrow from the neck to the forehead of any long-haired Britisher he caught. The sight of a dignified German colonel standing in the open, absorbed in this work, was ludicrous in the extreme, but he made such a mess of his next victims that they were glad to visit the barber's of their own accord and have the job completed.

I felt, as I told my host this story, that my French was too poor to do it justice, but despite my limitations, he seemed to appreciate it hugely. Then, as our digestive juices settled down to cope with the unwonted burden of responsibility we had just bestowed upon them, a feeling of delightful languor came over us, and I was content to sit dreamily watching the orderly as he busily collected the debris of the feast and paused every few moments to swat some of the myriads of flies, which had persisted in sharing our delight and were still buzzing happily over the fragments of food remaining.

Labeste was a pork butcher by trade. And while I watched him bestowing enough strength in the squashing of each fly to lay low the toughest old hog that ever grunted in France, I remember reflecting upon his wisdom in obtaining so secure a staff job under the protecting shadow of the church. Poor old Labeste! The date was 9 July 1916, and on 5 August I saw him marching away in a gang of prisoners destined to the torture of the German mines. Even the church was unable to protect its servants. Nobody was safe in Rennbahn from the menace of *Arbeit* (work) for the enemy.

Chapter 10

Escapes

I remember that about the time of my memorable feast with M. Manen we were all very excited, French, British, and Russians alike – the idea of escape loomed large in our minds. Twelve Frenchmen and two English had escaped from the camp together one night by means of a successful tunnel. I remember that the Englishmen were recaptured within twenty-four hours, and we never heard of any of the party reaching a neutral frontier, but the affair gave us encouragement.

The desire for freedom was ever present in the minds of nine out of ten prisoners. By day, whispers of secret schemes ran round among trusted friends. By night, our dreams were of ropes and ladders, of tunnels and of murdered sentries. As wild birds, caged, flutter about, ever trying to find a space between the bars, so with caged men. Ill treatment and starvation react on some natures by intensifying the desire for freedom, on others by rendering it dull and stupid. But Death alone can kill it. Scratched in a conspicuous place on a wooden wall in the camp were the words, *'Vive la fuite!'* ('Here's to liberty!') and the yearning thus expressed was common to us all. Conditions of captivity were unbearable and most prisoners who like myself had been captured unwounded, no matter how they braved it out, felt disgrace in having surrendered. We had sold liberty for life, and there were times when we repented of the bargain. To escape would be an expression of the feeling that we were still unconquered – it would level up our score against the hated enemy.

Escape from Rennbahn was, however, extremely difficult. It was natural that the authorities should do their best to discourage us. The *Lager* was built in such a way that all doors and windows opened on to the dreary barrack squares, and only from the gates and from one or two points in the camp could we obtain even a glimpse of the green country around us.

A triple girdle of wire surrounded the entire *Lager*, the most formidable barrier being a thick and close-meshed four-foot fence, which carried a high-voltage electric current. A yard on either side of this ran nine-foot barbed-wire fences. Guards patrolled this barrier continuously, and at night it was brilliantly illuminated by arc lamps at frequent intervals.

At first sight escape seemed impossible. Yet men did escape. Despite the difficulties, which seemed insuperable, despite the long lists, read out to us on parade, of prisoners killed and wounded in attempting flight from various German prisons, men fulfilled the yearning of their hearts – only, in the majority of cases to be recaptured. Brought back to the place they loathed, a sojourn in the cells under *strenger Arrest* awaited them. The punishment for a first offence was of only fourteen days' duration. But it was a bad fourteen days, for the cell was just large enough to contain one man. He could lie down in it, and he could stand up, but that was all. His bed was of straw, his bedding two thin cottony blankets, verminous and filthy; his food, a small ration of potato bread once daily; his drink, water. He was allowed to leave his cell thrice daily for five minutes in the open. To prevent his becoming mad, a skylight in the roof was removed on every third day to give him a few hours of light. And to prevent his death from hunger, he was allowed on these third days a bowl of soup in addition to his bread. Apart from these days of luxury, his time was spent in black darkness. In winter he came near death from cold in a space too limited for any exercise. In summer he stifled for want of air.

This was *strenger Arrest*. And it is significant of the life lived by prisoners of war in Germany that most of the men who endured this punishment thought little of it.

The first man to get out of Rennbahn during my time there was a French sergeant whose courage and ingenuity should have made his name live for ever in my memory, but I have forgotten it. In the winter of 1914 he had arrived in the camp, and in the early summer of 1915 he left it dramatically. I only knew him slightly. His garish red trousers and blue tunic made him appear a very ordinary Frenchman: but those who knew him well were aware that the resemblance to his fellows was only external – for he alone in the *Lager* wore two complete suits of clothing, the gaudy uniform hiding beneath it a civilian suit, the suit of a German workman, complete with the 'brassard' or armlet which enabled its wearer to enter and leave the camp unchallenged. I have often wondered how he obtained these; perhaps someone in the tailor's shop could tell the story, but the well-kept secret never reached me.

For months he wandered about the bare confines of the *Lager*, his mind centred upon the problem of finding the ideal moment for action. At last it came. A few German workmen visited us to make some repairs to the water system. They left two or three bicycles leaning against a hutment in Lagerstrasse, not far from the main gate, and began excavations near by, the sergeant watching from afar.

For some hours the work went on. And then some task called them all from Lagerstrasse into Block III. In a moment the Frenchman grasped the possibilities. Darting into his barrack, he tore off his scarlet bags and blue jacket, to emerge a few seconds later, a fair imitation of the better-class German artisan.

Without so much as a glance at the alluring bicycles, he strolled stolidly through the main gate, his brassard acting as Sesame. Once outside, he deliberately produced a long folding rule, and having made sundry measurements across the road and along an imaginary trench, and jotted down in his notebook a few figures, he shut up his rule and re-entered the gate. This time he made straight for the best of the bicycles, wheeled it calmly past the sentries and through the gate, mounted it, and pedalled quietly away. By nightfall he must have been half-way to the Dutch frontier. He never returned to tell us about it, but rumour goes that he abandoned the bicycle, and after a journey on foot across country, he swam a canal on the frontier under fire, and so won safety.

There was a buzz of excitement when this tale reached my barrack in Block IV, and one night soon afterwards a few of us put our heads together.

'There are only two possible ways out,' I declared after a long discussion. 'We can get out through the gates by some mixture of bluff and impudence like that French sergeant, or we can tunnel under the wire. To climb over the fences is impossible.'

'Well then,' said Hicky, 'Let us get out by the gate. We'll organise a few fellows to rush it.'

My knees wobbled at this idea. I thought of the guards in the block, the sentries at the block entrance, the patrols in Lagerstrasse, and the gate-guards. What would they be doing while we were working at the gate fastenings?

Coucher joined in. 'Wot I want to know,' he growled with his Cockney drawl, 'Why cawn't we get a hundred lads to have a bleedin' mutiny some night. Post a dozen in each block to down all the sentries, pinch the rifles, and switch out the lights. Then a round-up and a rush at the main gate.'

We considered this plan gravely before deciding it to be unworkable.

Black finally summed up the argument against it with a calm authority that settled the matter: 'There are spies in every room who would give the whole plot away. And if we did keep it secret, it could never be managed without some guard letting off his gun. Then you would have the soldiers marched in from the camp outside the maingate, and inside five minutes there would be a mowing down of English prisoners, and general hell for everyone in the camp.'

After this the conversation veered round to tunnels. We were in a kind of tunnel ourselves, half a dozen conspirators whispering together on mattresses in the darkest and stuffiest corner of the dark and stuffy room, our heads rubbing against the hammocks above, bulging under the bodies of sleeping men.

We let our imaginations build a glorious tunnel, dry and well timbered, securely hidden, with its exit well outside our barbed wire – a hole which might drain Rennbahn of all its bolder spirits. Our voices grew louder in our enthusiasm. Someone struck a match to light a cigarette, and our conversation was terminated like many of its kind by the gruff voice of one of the ever-watchful guards, ordering silence and bringing us back to the harsh realities of prison life. We turned into our lousy beds to dream of England.

A few weeks after this, four men in our room tried to make their dreams concrete. They pulled aside the mattress from this darkest corner, and using an ordinary pocket knife, they spent a day or two cutting out a square from the floor boards, making a hole just large enough for the biggest of them to squeeze through on to the sandy soil a couple of feet below.

We did not know how the work was proceeding nor what was going on, for they kept it very secret. Only the men who slept in their alley, and sometimes saw them emerge from the floor, hot and tired and filthy, knew that a tunnel was being made. The work was done by day, for it was impossible to get on with it without a little noise and, except on windy nights, sounds travel further and are more suspicious during the hours of darkness.

Then one morning Hicky came up to me, his eyes bright with a great idea. 'Jackson and his bunch have given up their tunnel scheme,' he told me. 'Let us carry on with it.'

'Yes, we are fed up with the whole damned thing,' declared Jackson when we asked him about it. 'Finish it if you can – but, for the love of Mike, let us know when you are hoping to break through, so that we can get out with you.'

My diary tells me that the date of this great excitement was 5 September 1915. Happy as sand larks, we prised up the trap and descended into the unknown region, between our floor and the earth, elbowing our way about on our stomachs until we found the vertical hole our friends had dug. It was some five feet deep, and at its base we could see the beginning of the tunnel. Hicky, being the smaller, crawled in to investigate, while I lay on top. My head over the side of the well, my heels scraping the floor boards, I peered down into the gloom and saw my friend's feet disappear.

After a few minutes they emerged again, and I looked down upon Hicky kneeling at the bottom of the hole. He was reeking with sweat and filthy beyond description. 'There's hell's own stink in there,' he whispered, when I had pulled him out. 'I'm about done in.'

I left him to recover and with the utmost difficulty curled myself round until my head and shoulders were in the tunnel and dragged myself forward. The word 'tunnel' immediately modified its meaning. This was not the tunnel of my dreams, cool, romantic, with timbered sides and roof. This thing which I had imagined as a road to freedom was just a black stinking death trap. Narrow and low at the opening, so that my shoulders seemed to fill it, the blackness inside was the tangible velvet of a tomb. It narrowed still further. I felt suffocated. There seemed no props to support the roof. I thought of the possibility of a collapse of sand, and panic seized me. I began to wriggle myself backwards, to emerge panting and exhausted and utterly disillusioned as to the glamour and romance of tunnel schemes.

Hicky was more courageous than I. He made a half-hearted attempt to enlarge the entrance, using a small and broken shovel our predecessors had bequeathed us and handing sand up to me in a little box to be scattered about on top.

We went down several days in succession, doing very little, but hating to give up the idea, more even than we hated the work. The moisture in the hole seemed to be increasing, and its stench made us suspect that it came from one of the camp sewers. Our clothing was so foul that we feared that it might lead to our detection. My distaste grew. I felt that it was better to be shot in the open than smothered in a sand-fall.

Hicky came to me one day with his usual cheery 'What about it?' and when I replied, 'To hell with it,' he added a fervent 'Amen'. Never again did we go through the floor.

Coucher and some other fellows tried to carry on. We made the same arrangement with them that Jackson had made with us, and we hoped for the best. But miners are born, not made, and this third combine was beaten by the bad air and general beastliness. They seemed to do very little work, and finally, declaring that they had struck oil or water or some viscous fluid and 'flooded the barstard', they gave it up altogether.

By this time everyone in the room knew that something had been going on, and the news soon went round, so that a man in Block I once asked me when we hoped to break through and seemed vastly disappointed when I told him there was nothing doing.

Then, in the evening of 25 September, just as we were going to bed, there entered a German officer accompanied by a *Feldwebel* and three armed guards, clumping up the alley straight towards the hidden trap door. I peeped apprehensively out of my blankets and saw the occupant of the corner bed turned out. His mattress was pulled aside, and the *Feldwebel* dropped on his knees examining the boards in the beam of his electric torch. In no time sounds indicative of German satisfaction and a burst of indignant muttering announced the discovery of the cut floor. A bayonet point was thrust into the nick, and out came the planks. Down went the *Feldwebel*, to return triumphant.

'*Raus!*'

Amid the usual schweinerings and hustlings and menaces, out we had to go, scarcely given time to pull on our trousers. I was sleeping in mine, so I remember being able to get out decently, but others were not so fortunate, and a funny sight they looked as we all stood shivering in the square, while our quarters were searched and the floor firmly nailed down.

At 4.00am next morning we were 'rousted' again to enjoy more of this 'still standing' and to listen to the harangue of the German sergeant-major, who through an interpreter threatened us with stoppage of all letters and parcels, unless the mining engineers would own up.

Hicky and I were urged by some of our comrades to confess. But we declared that having neither begun the tunnel nor finished it and indeed done nothing more than look at it, we could not be expected to act as scapegoats. Coucher took up the same attitude. Jackson and his party had gone 'on *Kommando*', hoping to get an opportunity of escape from some other *Lager*, and none of us felt inclined to upset their plans by the mention of their names.

The situation seemed at an impasse, and I don't know how long we should have been kept standing still if Coucher had not taken all the burden of crime on his own broad shoulders and been marched off, grinning and joking, for a fortnight's 'clink'.

This incident taught me a lesson. I now realised that the presence of spies among us was no mere romantic fancy, but a proven fact. How otherwise could we account for the manner in which the search party had gone direct to the right spot?

Spies or no spies, however, ours was not the last tunnel to be dug at Rennbahn, and on one occasion months afterwards, in the summer of 1916, I remember the pipe major describing his block to me as being 'like a suckin' rabbit warren'.

'We have a grand tunnel right out from under where you are sitting,' he told me as we sat smoking our pipes together in his room. 'Pat, that blaspheming old devil of a thieving Irishman over there, is the chief engineer. And there's a fine morning coming very soon when the old square-heads won't find an Englishman left in this block.'

Alas for the best laid plans of men and mice!

Pat and his friends, unable to speak a word of German, invited a French interpreter to go with them. It seemed a silly idea to me, for I saw only danger in an escaping prisoner attempting the language, unless he were dressed to act the German perfectly as well. And Coltan, the interpreter, was a resplendent individual who swaggered about among us decked out in a Belgian cavalry uniform complete with glittering spurs. He was all spit and polish, and I distrusted him.

A week or so later Pat told me how the plans had gone agley. He was a jolly fellow, one of the best of the regular soldiers that I knew, but I found him very down in the mouth.

'It was that ****** interpreter let us down,' he said. 'The ******* turned up on the night we had fixed for the break-through, wearing his bleedin' spurs, and nothing we could say would make him leave them behind. Evans and Harrison went first, about 1.00am last Monday morning. Then old Coltan's nerve failed him, and we had to threaten to twist his neck before we got him pushed into the hole. I waited about five minutes before I followed him, and then half way along I bumped my nose on his sucking spurs, and I had the devil's job to get him to keep on crawling. Finally, when we got to the outlet, he stuck his head out for a moment and then shuffled back again, corking up the hole so that I could not pass him. He would not budge and said something about a German sentry close by. If I had had a bayonet I might have shifted him on, but, after a lot of muckin' about, back we had to come. It was nearly morning by this time, so I gave it up.'

'Why did you not have a go the next night?' I asked. 'Too much moon ever since,' he answered.

'And what of Evans and Harrison?'

'Oh – they got clear away all right, but Sanders at the post office tells me they have been caught again.'

Poor old Pat! Next time he tried the sap, he found it silted up and impassable, and he had no heart to excavate again.

Although the pipe major's description of his block as a rabbit warren was an exaggeration, there were a good many tunnels in the *Lager* at one time and another. One digging party came to the surface too soon and emerged just on the wrong side of the wire. Another burrowed too near the surface so that a horse and cart broke through it.

But the sapper who had the hardest luck of all was a man named Watson, the pioneer of all this activity. It was he who made the first tunnel away back in the summer of 1915, a substantial passage from under his barrack in Block II, fifteen to twenty yards long, some four feet below ground.

Ill luck dogged his labours, for just as he was approaching their completion, Block II was cleared of all its inhabitants and closed.

Watson would not be beaten. He managed to continue the job and still to keep it so secret that none of us knew of it, except one or two of his intimates. I heard afterwards that he used to crawl daily along a ditch that led from Querstrasse, the easterly cross-road of the camp, under the huts near the spot where his sap began. And then he was seen by a sentry and ordered out, covered by a rifle.

His fourteen days punishment completed, Watson, two days later, was reported missing. He had gone to work with a fatigue party to some stables near Münster and had managed to avoid returning with the party by concealing himself under a pile of straw. But again luck was against him. He was discovered soon afterwards by a farmer who handed him over to the police, and he returned to the *Lager* next day between two guards.

A short time elapsed between this ignominious return and his trial, and in the meantime he was free to roam about the camp. On hearing that another tunnel was nearing its last stages of perfection, he asked the British sergeants who were working it whether he might use it too, and on the night before the day fixed for his trial, he vanished again.

Except that he returned under escort once more a few days later. I know nothing of his adventures, for he was taken straight to the cells. And when he came out of clink he was sent away to some camp in Eastern Prussia, and we knew of him no more.

Another man I remember, possessed of the same indomitable will to escape at all costs, was a youngster named Marris, who thrice rode out of the camp unseen and thrice returned, and the Germans know nothing about it to this day.

A small frail-looking lad was Marris; in fact he was physically only a portion of an Englishman, for a German shell had torn out two or three of his ribs and left a great hole in his side. He had been a prisoner in a camp near Berlin and had managed to get out of it dressed in a civilian suit he had borrowed for the occasion. Speaking perfect German, he had boldly purchased a ticket at the railway station for some West-phalian town, boarded a train which he knew went to Holland, and sat tight, hoping to be able to get under a seat when near the frontier. Unfortunately for him, he was unable to find an empty compartment, and since he had no passport, he was hauled out at some frontier town and re-interned at Münster, to endure the usual happy fortnight in cells.

After this he was appointed as an interpreter, for he was recognised as physically unfit for work, and he acted for some months as a buffer between oppressors and oppressed, often finding himself in trouble for championing the cause of the weak. After a while he got very restive and cast about for some way of reaching home. Original in most things, his method of leaving the camp was perhaps the most original of all his doings.

A cart left the *Lager* almost every day laden with empty sacks and cases destined for Hiltrup station, two or three kilometres to the south of Rennbahn, and returned after discharging its load with a supply of parcels and stores. Marris, being small, smuggled himself one day into the bottom of this cart, while the sergeant in charge of the British parcels office covered him with sacks and boxes. And so he left the camp, the sentries, who watched the cart rumble along the wood-paved road out of the *Lager*, as ignorant as the armed guards, who accompanied it, of the fact that it contained a pale-faced, great-spirited little *Engländer*. The British fatigue party who walked beside the vehicle were to rap on the side immediately a chance occurred for the unseen passenger to leave it unobserved. But no chance came, and he had to remain in the cart while it was emptied and reloaded, returning to Rennbahn stiff and uncomfortable under a heavy burden of parcels.

Thrice he went through this ordeal. Then, in desperation, he made friends with the men who carried the big refuse bins to the pigs at the farm outside the *Lager*. I was told that they carried him out, buried up to the neck in pig swill, but it seems more likely that his journey was made in an empty bin. It was a pity that the guard was looking when he was emptied out, for it must have given him a shock to see Englishmen giving a comrade to be devoured by the pigs.

After this he was sent on *Kommando*; Libau in Poland was his destination, if camp gossip was correct.

The daring and impudence of the French sergeant who cycled away from Rennbahn was equalled later on by one of his comrades, who simply ran out. This man, who spoke fluent German, had noticed that a large party of prisoners were usually marched into camp daily at about 3.30pm from the hospital just outside the West Gate. So he made a habit of strolling in that direction with a few friends at about the time the party was expected and fraternising with the sentry there. One day it chanced that the German on duty proved to be an exceptionally slow moving, sleepy old fellow, and the Frenchman knew that his chance had come.

In due course the expected column made its appearance. The guard slung his rifle over his shoulder and began to fumble with the gate fastenings.

'Keep him talking about his beloved *Vaterland*,' whispered the Frenchman to his friends, as they drew aside to allow the incomers to pass.

The last man entered. The sentry was slowly shutting the heavy gate. Suddenly a shadow darted past him through the narrowing gap, and in a second, light footed as a mountain goat, the Frenchman had leaped across the road and vanished among the trees opposite, before the shaking guard had unslung his rifle.

When I heard this story from Devignes, a trombone player I knew in the French symphony orchestra, I scarcely believed it and asked my trusty teacher and pupil Adjutant Dacros whether it was true.

'But yes, my friend,' he assured me. 'I knew the light-footed one very well. We Frenchmen have ze imagination, ze enterprise; you Engleesh have ze tunnels.'

He chuckled for a long time at this cheap witticism, and then he told me a story which was even more amusing and assured me that he had seen the incident himself. It had happened in the late afternoon just before the blocks were closed, and there had been very few witnesses.

In the potato field adjacent to the southern boundary of our camp, a long file of Russian prisoners were working listlessly under the rather negligent eyes of two guards, who were lulled into a sense of security by the dejected appearance of their wards. One or two very fat German women were stooping with them, weeding and hoeing drearily and mechanically. The whole line of toilers seemed devoid of interest in anything, moving together like a slow machine. Ducros was watching them idly, reflecting on the misery of these Russians, for whom even the return home would mean little better than the exchange of one serfdom for another, when he noticed the most ragged of the wretched band, who was next in the line to the fattest of the German ladies, slowly straighten his aching back and stretch himself. Then, suddenly galvanised into a surprising manifestation of energetic activity, his heavy boot drove straight at the bulkiest portion of the stooping dame beside him, flopping her forward on to her face. Having thus demonstrated his feelings towards Germans and Germany, before even his violent kick had taken full effect, he was leaping and plunging at express speed towards a wood near by. A comrade followed at his heels, rags and tatters fluttering behind them in the wind. Bang! Bang! went the guards' rifles. Bang! Bang! again from the sentries at the camp gate. But still the ragged figures bounded on and, reaching the wood, disappeared.

Two hoes without owners, four dejected guards, four dirty rifles, and one squealing old woman were all that remained to show that the thing had happened.

Ducros began telling me all this in his laboured English, but before he was halfway through, he got so interested that he lapsed into a flow of rapid French that I had difficulty in following.

For the first time I realised that under their ragged greatcoats some of these Russkies had imagination, and a few months after this, Ivan Eldik, a Dutch guard I met in Holland, told me of another Russian escape that showed how misleading the abject appearance of these grey-coated scarecrows might be. It was a desperate affair.

A party of some fifteen Russkies were employed on a German farm within a few kilometres of the Dutch frontier. Their guards, presuming that these ignorant barbarians from the North would have no idea of their proximity to Holland and despising their charges for their slowness and dumb passivity, treated them brutally, dealing out kicks and blows with heavy boots and clubbed rifles, never dreaming of possible retribution. But among the victims was one from Poland who knew German and who was able to gather from the gibes and laughter of the guards the direction and approximate distance of the frontier. They plotted and waited and continued to suffer injuries and insults in silence, until one stormy night they suddenly attacked their bullies. They were big men and although some of the Germans were spitted on their own bayonets, most of them had the life crushed from their throats by powerful hairy hands.

Then began a steady march through the night, which in a few hours brought the little band into Holland.

It was not so uncommon for men to get away from working parties as from our settled camp with its impassable electric barrier, its arc lamps, and its host of sentries, and many of my friends volunteered gaily for *Kommando* with the sole object of finding an opportunity of legging it. There was a big risk in doing this, for it was a step which might take a man months or years of toil and torment from which no escape could be contrived, and which after a few weeks might make such a wreck of him that he would have neither heart nor strength for any tours through Germany.

A Canadian named Stubbs, who managed to get away from a mine near Dortmund, had a heart-breaking experience. I shall never forget Stubbs. He was a striking looking man, small in build, but conspicuous because of his great mop of glowing red hair and for a mischievous twinkle that danced perpetually in his merry grey eyes. And the twinkle was still dancing when he returned to us in Rennbahn after his break away.

'Guess I've had a grand piece of walkin', he said cheerily after his return in the spring of 1916. He had actually been in Holland. After some seven or eight days, during which he had travelled only in the hours of darkness and spent the rest of the time hiding, there came one morning when he saw labourers busy in the fields ahead, so he retraced his steps to a wood through which he had passed and fell asleep on a bed of leaves and branches. His slumber was rudely disturbed a few hours later by a couple of German frontier guards, who marched him off to the nearest railway station to be returned for trial. The bitterness of the experience lay in the fact that the frontier line passed through the wood, and he had chosen his sleeping place a hundred yards or so on the wrong side of it. As for the labourers, the sight of whom had caused his retreat – these were Dutchmen tilling the peaceful fields of Holland!

Chapter 11

Preparations for Escape

The summer of 1916 was an evil time for us. *Le cafard* (lit. cockroach; slang: melancholy, depression) was busy. One or two men went mad. Quarrels, even fights occurred. I had a bad dose of toothache and earache in July and, by ill-luck, during one of my specially bad nights, old Tommy Deslie, a Scots Canadian whom everybody loved, got hold of a bottle of schnapps. He was a rip-snortin', rollicking, devil-may-care mass of good nature, and he had a way with him that won smiles from even the guards.

I don't know where he held his revels that night, but it was not until about 4.00am that he came in to bed and wakened all the inmates of Room 2 by the most godless mixture of 'Scots Wha Hae' and 'Annie Laurie' that I had ever heard.

'Put a sock in it, Tommy,' I groaned, wishing that Englishmen had been born without teeth and Scotsmen without thirst.

He strode over and grinned at me. 'Did ye no like ma singin'?' he bawled. 'I'll gie ye a new hymn the noo.' There followed a dolorous ditty concerning a virtuous young woman of Chippey town, who was 'looking for her man, who was doing her wrong'. Then he came and tickled my toes in great good spirits.

'Tommy,' I said, 'if you do that again, I'll punch your ugly face.'

He laughed uproariously at this – he had been 'chucker out' in some Wild West saloon during one period of his chequered career – and, grasping the foot of my wooden bedstead, he upended it until I was beginning to slither out on to my head. Then he let it down with a bang.

This was too much for a man half-mad with toothache. Out I jumped in my shirt and landed a stinging flat-hander over the side of his jaw.

Round the room and to and fro we fought, upsetting boxes and breaking beds. Somebody's larder came down with a crash. I forgot my tooth and began to wish I had put on my boots and socks before opening hostilities. My toe hit something hard. I remember that. And then, without my being aware of any lapse of time, I felt a scorching sensation in my throat and found that I was on my back among a lot of wreckage with Deslie leaning over me and pouring neat schnapps into my mouth.

'Losh mon!' he yelled. 'What a hell of a crash ye went! I thocht I had killed ye. Here! Take hand o' the bottle yersel. There's no but a wee drappie. Sup the lot.'

I took this kindly advice and, finding myself none the worse, I rejoiced that my toothache had vanished.

It is no matter for surprise that some of us became nervy and morose at this period. We were beginning to realise that the war might be a long one. News bulletins supplied by the Germans continued to rejoice in their stupendous victories over the Russians. We were repeatedly assured that London had been destroyed by air raids, and as from time to time Zeppelins sailed overhead, we wondered whether there might be any truth in the enemies' statements. It was seldom that we could obtain any cheering news. Even an English newspaper smuggled past the parcels censorship gave little comfort. Kut had fallen in the spring, and Serbia had been reduced to the condition of Belgium. Day after day the flags fluttered gaily above the *Kommandantur*, and as the spirits of our guards rose, it seemed to us that their aggressiveness increased.

The state of our friends on working parties distressed us. Men drifted back to the *Lager* in twos and threes, broken on the wheel of German industry, and the stories they told of German brutality appalled us. Charlie Black had been shot by a guard for throwing down his tools at some coke oven near Dortmund. The bullet, fortunately of light calibre, was cut out of his flesh without the employment of any anaesthetic whatever, and Charlie was roughly bound up and ordered to get to work again the following day. Later on, however, he had become seriously ill and had been drafted back to Münster as being of no further use.

The bodies of these men on *Kommando* were worn out and broken, but their pluck was amazing. Riach of the Durhams told of a friend of his working with him near Chemnitz. When a guard, whom this man had angered, whipped out a revolver and pointed it at his chest, he took off his old battle-scarred khaki cap and hung it on the pistol muzzle, laughing in the German's face.

I was sitting near the East Gate one afternoon a few days after my scrap with Deslie, musing upon the hopeless condition of prisoners of war and wondering whether the misery of men on working parties was not to be preferred to the deadly stagnation and depression of this sheltered Rennbahn existence. A small stretch of green country was visible through the barbed wire, and one or two German civilians, who came wandering along a path nearby, paused to gaze curiously at the caged *Engländer*, peering and pointing at me like visitors to a zoo. Earlier in my captivity, I should have moved away, embarrassed and uncomfortable under their curious scrutiny. But now I felt utterly indifferent. I must be getting *abruti* (degraded to the brute level, moronic), I reflected. What did they matter, these German strollers? What did anything matter? I seemed to be losing all interest in life. How long, O Lord? How long would this weary waiting continue? I must get out of it somehow! Escape! Yet what was the use trying it? Of the few men who had managed to get away from Rennbahn, how many had succeeded in reaching England? Not one. A few French, perhaps a couple of Russians had won through to Holland – but all our English schemes had been bubbles, with those Britishers who had escaped from the camp having been invariably brought back.

The sound of a mighty oath disturbed my musings, and a Canadian voice uttered the thought that was in my mind. '********! Guess it's time we got on the other side of those god-darned fences!'

Turning my head, I saw that the speaker was Gerrie Burk, a Canadian who had been captured at Ypres the same time as myself.

'And when in hell and how in hell are we going to get there?' I exclaimed bitterly. 'It's no use taking a running jump at the gate; and if talking about escape were any good, we should all be out of Germany now.'

Gerrie sat down and began filling his pipe. 'What about starting in with a little tunnel?' he drawled.

The word tunnel set my teeth on edge. 'I don't know very much about tunnels,' I said, 'but what I do know is enough. There's no tunnelling for me.'

I told him how Hicky and I had amused ourselves in Room 9 the previous autumn. Then a young air mechanic joined us – 'Flieger' we called him – and the three of us spent the rest of the afternoon trying to devise some means of getting on the right side of that wire.

Flieger's mind was full of a hair-brained scheme to sneak down to the aerodrome at Münster and to steal a German plane. 'I could manage a Taube quite well,' he assured us. 'And it would be a darned sight easier to fly than to walk.'

'Aw, Hell!' muttered Gerrie disgustedly. 'I guess I got a better notion than that! Stop up all the doors and windows in Room 2. Get Flieger talking until the whole darned place is fall of gas and hot air; and then away we'll go – the room and all, like the old son of a gun in the fairy story with his carpet.'

'But, man! – an aeroplane would get us to England in a few hours,' exclaimed the mechanic excitedly, raising his voice to such a yell that the surly old sentry at the gate glanced at us suspiciously.

Gerry looked round anxiously. 'Guess we had better beat it right now,' he said. 'That lop-eared, cross-eyed old sauerkraut at the gate looks interested in your high-flyin' notions, Flieger.'

We moved away to continue the discussion in whispers far into the night. And Burk and I carried on the topic the next day, and the next, evolving plans and discarding them as hopeless.

'Look here!' I said to him one morning a few days later. 'A couple of Frenchmen broke away from their parcels fatigue a few weeks ago.'

'Yes. I have been on that job myself,' replied Gerry. 'It's never any use on the British fatigue. The guards keep too close a watch. Besides, a guy has a poor chance of making Holland if he has no food with him. And you can't take much food to Hiltrup on fatigue.'

I agreed. 'But I'll tell you what, Gerry. We're both as stale as can be. I've never been outside this damned camp since Billson came back from Münster gaol, and I'm going to volunteer for a job with our Hiltrup party. Come on and see Sergeant Derry and fix it up now.'

It was easily arranged. We went to Hiltrup next day, yoked like horses to a great cart with about a dozen other British prisoners. I remember that it rained all the time – but it was good to stretch our legs and we enjoyed the experience.

We had a grand feed on our return; and as I ate, my thoughts ran perpetually on the all absorbing question of escape. Suddenly an idea struck me. 'Gerrie!' I cried, 'There's no electricity through the wire on the gates.' I spoke so sharply that my friend almost dropped the Nestle's milk tin from which he was drinking.

'********', he drawled! 'You sure startled me some. I guess you've made a real big discovery.'

'I've discovered more than you think,' I muttered, nettled at his sarcastic tone. 'All we have to do is to pick a wet and windy night, crawl up to one of the gates, cut the wire underneath it with some strong scissors, and crawl through.'

We hurriedly finished our meal and then went out together to examine the four camp gates. Three were quite useless for our purpose, but the fourth, the West Gate, near the hospital, looked hopeful. There was a space of nearly eighteen inches between its bottom bar and the ground, protected only by two sagging strands of barbed wire.

The sentry eyed us sullenly as we looked at it.

'We could stay in old Duff's room in Block I till late afternoon,' I suggested – 'and get under his floor; he has a hole all ready made for the job. All we would have to do would be to lie doggo until dark, crawl under the huts to the point nearest this gate, and keep an eye on this sentry. Then, when the wind and rain drove him into his box, away we could go.'

'We would be missed from the evening roll call in Block IV before we were out of the camp,' objected Gerrie.

'Well,' I replied. 'They would never think of looking for us under a floor in Block I.'

But I could see that my friend did not like my scheme. 'Suppose the wind dropped and the stars came out,' he said. 'You can't tell what this ******* German weather will do until it does it. And the sentry that night might be a leathery-skinned old guy, who likes rain and wind and never uses his box.'

I felt the truth of these objections, but obviously there was no getting out of Rennbahn without taking chances, and finally, for want of a better plan, we decided on this one. Our preparations began to make headway. Almost every day we tramped to Hiltrup in an attempt to accustom our legs to walking and to get ourselves into better physical trim.

We bartered jellies and sweets and books and cakes for French army blankets and meat cubes. We hoarded chocolate. Our pile of provisions grew amazingly.

'I don't know how we are going to carry this lot with us to Holland, Gerrie,' I said one day as we went to add a bully-beef tin to the stock.

The Canadian had a brain wave. 'We want some pockets,' he said. 'If we had a spare shirt each, we could make slits up the sides, double up the front and the tails, and stitch them up so as to make waistcoats full of pockets. I know a guy in the tailor's shop who would do them both for a few marks, and he would keep his mouth shut too.'

We found two strong flannel shirts, and within a few days they were returned to us reconstructed as we desired. They were even better than our expectations, each containing eight pockets in front and four behind. We were so jubilant that we showed them to Billson and

Hicky, taking them both into our confidence. They thought the patent waistcoats a great idea, but I could see that they were dubious as regards our proposed attempt to crawl under the West Gate.

'The sentry box is right up against it,' said Billson.

I saw his face cloud with anxiety and feared he was going to act as a wet blanket, but his genial smile reappeared in a few seconds.

'Have you a water-bottle?' he demanded.

When we admitted that we had none, he immediately went over to his old kit bag and produced his own army bottle, a treasured relic of the battlefield. 'Take this,' he said. 'You'll want it.'

The spontaneous gift of that bottle was a mark of that real generosity which stamps a man as pure gold. He would miss it badly, and he would never be able to replace it.

Hicky was interested in routes and distances to Holland. 'Have you a map?' he asked. 'Guess we just make west until we find some windmills,' replied Gerry, asking how he reckoned we could get luxuries like maps in Rennbahn.

Hicky shook his head. 'You ought to have a map,' he said, and he suggested that M. Allée, the senior French adjutant of the *Lager*, might be able to help us.

I went to see this gentleman at once. To my surprise, he agreed to obtain both a map and a compass for me, but he would not drop the least hint as to how or where he hoped to get them.

'Zey will cost me 3 marks each,' he said smiling. 'If you have not ze money, you shall pay me *après la guerre*.'

Inside a week we had the map and compass. The map was a beauty, although on rather a small scale for a walking tour; and as soon as I received it, I set to work at my rough table in Room 2 making a careful copy of the section between Münster and the Dutch frontier and marking out our proposed route.

I was so engrossed in my task that I nearly came to grief over it, for while working I suddenly heard the voice of a guard outside. Hurriedly I drew a number of loose papers and a book over my plan as the German entered the room.

Something in my manner or perhaps some anxiety of expression must have attracted his attention, for he came over to me and gruffly inquired what I was doing.

'*Was tun sie?*' (What are you doing?) he demanded suspiciously. '*Ich lese*' (I am reading).

I tried hard to sound indifferent and resisted a mad desire to pull more papers over my precious contraband. '*Was lesen sie?*' (What are you reading?) persisted the German.

'Geography,' I hazarded, amused in the midst of my concern, at the irony of my reply. 'Ah! Geography!' His tone changed from one of suspicion to a patronising satisfaction.

'*Zo! Gut!*' And away he trotted, leaving me to continue my studies.

The day after this episode – my diary records it as 9 August – our plans were even more seriously jeopardised. More than half the members of our Students Society were notified that they were to leave Münster next morning to proceed to a working camp in Poland, and Gerrie's name was included in the list of condemned.

His language did credit to the situation. Canadian swearing usually amused me tremendously, but on this occasion I was too upset to listen to it. I left him addressing the world and hurried round to Derry, the senior English sergeant in the block.

'Have you anything to do with this list of men for Poland?' I stormed at him. 'Not a bit,' he assured me. 'They want eighty men though. What's the trouble?'

I poured out our troubles, and when I told him of our plans to escape, he promised to attempt to have Burk's name deleted from the list on grounds of ill health, but he warned me that it would be wise for my fellow conspirator to keep out of the way next morning.

August 10th opened badly. Soon after midnight some of us were roused from sleep by the report of a rifle. Billson cursed us for chattering about it.

'Get to sleep,' he growled. 'It's only one of the sentries accidently shooting his foot to save him from going to the front.' – but we were to hear another explanation a few hours later.

We students in Room 2 were usually treated with just a trace of courtesy by our guards, but on that morning of 10 August, we were 'rousted' with unnecessary violence and kept standing on parade for a long time after roll call. Then our *Feldwebel* came on the scene with orders that the Libau party was to leave within an hour.

'Gerry,' I said, as the parade dismissed, 'we will have to have a quick breakfast and get out of this "toot sweet" to Block I.'

Kohn, our block interpreter, came in while we were eating. 'Did you hear that shot last night?' he asked. 'It just about blew the tripes out of a little Froggie.'

I looked up wondering for a moment what he meant, and when I saw his serious expression, I realised he had meant his words to be taken literally.

'Do you mean that a Frenchman has been shot?' demanded Gerrie.

Kohn explained. He had just been talking to one of the *Feldwebels* with whom, both being Jews, he was on comparatively good terms, and had obtained the whole story with a great wealth of detail.

Ten Frenchmen had tried to escape from the *Lager* during the night. They had crawled through a passage they had scraped under the huts from our block to the no man's land on the camp borders and had lain hidden in a potato bed just inside the wire. Keeping perfectly motionless while sentries were passing and working hard when the coast seemed clear, they scraped and dug to make a trench under the triple girdle that separated them from freedom.

It was a long and dangerous task, for a touch on the middle fence would have meant death, and sentries kept passing within a few yards of them. Thanks to the excellence of their potato screen they escaped detection, for the moaning of the night wind swallowed up any small noises they made, and in a few hours they had scraped away enough sandy soil to allow them passage. Nine of them were at last crawling snake fashion through the field outside the camp. But the clothing of the tenth, who was hampered by a rucksack of food on his back, caught on the barbs of the inner fence.

His sensations can be imagined as he lay pinned upon his back, his face under the deadly centre wire, white in the glare of the arc lamps, his feet still among the friendly potato plants. He could hear a sentry's step approaching. He tried to pull himself free. The barbed wire jangled but still held him. He tugged again.

The sentry heard a noise at the wire. He saw it bending and moving. He hurried through the potato plants to find one of the accursed *Gefangeners* caught in the very act of escaping. Instead of pulling him back again, he thrust his rifle muzzle through the wire until the bayonet point touched his victim's chest, and pulled the trigger.

I felt sick at Kohn's story – there were no potatoes to screen us at the West Gate – but my partner seemed unimpressed.

'That god-darned son of the *Vaterland* meant business all right,' he said lightly. And then I remember his hurried continuation of breakfast and his 'Guess we had better beat it out of here right now,' that marked its completion.

We managed to avoid the *Kommando*. It marched off at 5.30am, seventy-nine strong instead of eighty – Sergeant Derry had done the trick for us.

Later in the day, I was attracted by a few prisoners staring at our block notice board and strolled over to see what was absorbing their interest. It was a special advertisement in three languages, pinned adjacent to the usual list of prisoners shot while attempting to escape from other camps. It invited all and sundry to inspect the corpse of the morning's victim and expressed the pious hope that his fate would be a warning to the whole camp.

I did not accept this invitation. Instead, I strolled along to the West Gate once more with Burk and looked at it long and pensively.

'Gerry,' I said. 'That sentry box is less than four yards from the gate.'

He grinned. 'Those soft-nosed, heavy-calibre German bullets sure make a full-sized hole where they come out. There will have to be a hell of a storm of wind the night we go if we are to get away without lead poisoning.' We turned and made our way back to our block in silence.

Chapter 12

We Leave Camp

By the middle of August our preparations were complete. We were each equipped with map and compass, our boots were well nailed, our patent waistcoats hidden under our barrack floor, stuffed with concentrated foods.

We could have made the attempt then, but since we had agreed that the journey to Holland must be made entirely by night, we waited for the hours of darkness to lengthen a little.

Meanwhile some of our friends, whose health had been permanently broken by conditions on *Kommando*, had been transferred from the *Lager* to the *Lazarett* (hospital) just outside. Among these sick men were Charlie Black and two Canadians, Wilson and Cleeton, special pals of Burk's.

My fellow plotter came to me one day towards the end of August, his face beaming in a way I always associated with some unusual mental activity.

'I've just been to see Wilson and Cleeton in the *Lazarett*,' he announced. 'How on earth did you manage to get in?' I asked. 'I thought – '

'Easy,' interrupted Gerrie. 'The sentry at West Gate happened to know a bit of English, and when I explained that I had some books and things for them, he just opened the gate and in I went. I noticed that the god-darned old son of a sausage-maker kept his gun pointing in my direction till I was past his pal at the *Lazarett* gate, but that didn't worry me any.'

He paused for breath, and I wondered what was coming. 'Have you ever been in the *Lazarett*?' he went on. I shook my head.

'Say! It's a dandy place to get out of. There's just one ten-foot barbed-wire fence round it, two or three guards, and a dog. We could climb over the wire easy! It's a cinch!'

'That fence is pretty well lit up at night,' I objected. 'And ten feet of close-meshed barbed wire is a hell of a thing to step over in a hurry. There's the dog too.'

'Shucks man!' he retorted impatiently. 'It's no better lit up than your West Gate. And as for the dog, we can stick a knife into the – '

I was impressed by his enthusiasm and agreed to accompany him on a reconnaissance next day.

The guards made little demur about allowing us passage, and as soon as we had passed them, I saw that my friend's idea was a good one. The hospital enclosure was a rough square on a side of some thirty yards, and in it were three long barracks which served as wards for the most serious cases of sickness in the camp.

On entering one of these buildings we found it occupied by some twenty men, cheery enough and elated at the possibility of being sent to Holland or Switzerland on some 'exchange of prisoners' scheme. Most of them were heart and lung cases, and some were suffering from old wounds. The gravity of their illnesses was not immediately apparent, for although none looked well, there were few of them bedridden.

Our three special friends gave us a cordial greeting, and when we broached our plans to them, they were eager to help us.

'What troubles me most,' I told them, 'is the dog.' Cleeton laughed.

'Never worry about him,' he exclaimed. 'He's a great pal of mine. If you two can get over the wire, Wilson and I will get over the dog for you.'

My spirits rose.

'Gerry,' I said. 'Let's have a look at that ten-foot fence.'

It looked formidable enough, but we found that at a point furthest from the gates, a strong beam cut diagonally from the base of one post to the top of the next one.

I pointed this out to my partner. We could climb up this support one after the other, holding the top wire lightly to keep our balance, stand on the top for a second, and leap down to the other side.

'It's just a toss-up as to whether one of the sentries sees us or not,' said Gerrie. 'If that god-darned poodle starts yapping round our heels, I guess their all-fired curiosity will get the better of them, and one of them will come and ask us why we aren't in bed.'

I followed the direction of his gaze. The poodle had his eyes fixed on us malevolently. It was a huge Alsatian, chained near its kennel less than twenty yards from us.

'I wonder whether they keep him chained at night,' I muttered anxiously.

'I reckon if Cleeton says he'll fix him, he'll fix him all right,' replied my friend cheerily. On our return to Block IV we had definitely abandoned the gate-crawling plan in favour of this less dangerous alternative. If once we could get away from Rennbahn, we thought we should be comparatively free from danger until near the frontier. Travelling by night across country and hiding by day, we reckoned that we ought to be in Holland in about five days.

Clothes bothered us a little. Our khaki had perished completely, and we were garbed in ill-fitting black suits rendered hideously conspicuous by broad stripes of yellow cloth which had been 'let in' down the sides of the trousers and the backs of the coats. Since we could think of no means of hiding these tell-tale stripes, we hoped to travel absolutely unseen, avoiding all roads and giving towns and villages as wide a berth as possible.

I was a little uneasy, too, about my partner's powers of physical endurance, for some months of German coke ovens had left his heart groggy. He must have felt disquietude himself, for he bought a bottle of crème de menthe, the strongest liqueur we could obtain.

I laughed when he showed this to me.

'Would not schnapps have been better?' I asked.

'No sir,' he replied. 'The peppermint flavour is better than any schnapps. And if that stuff is not strong enough for you, what do you say to this?'

He pulled out from under his jacket a second bottle. To my surprise I found it labelled 'Pure Alcohol'. 'Where in hell did you get this?' I gasped.

'I just went in to the block hospital and got that old medical orderly pal of yours to sound my chest. Told him I had a pain in my guts. And while he was putting away his tubes, I managed to put this under my coat before I left.'

'But we can't take two thundering great bottles like that with us!' I ejaculated.

Gerrie laughed. 'We will pour half of each down a drain, then mix up the remainder in one bottle. And I guess we shall have a tonic that would bring a dead man back to life again.'

We got rid of half the alcohol via the drain, but the crème de menthe was too good to waste that way, and we gave away what we did not want.

We had decided to make our break on the night of Tuesday, 5 September, and to make for the Dutch frontier at a point near the town of Enschede.

Our secret had been well kept. Except for Billson, Hicky, Flieger, and M. Allée in the *Lager* and the three men in the hospital, not a soul knew of our project. We had no fears of any of these men spreading the news, but we were on pins and needles to be off, now that we had worked out a more or less detailed scheme. The nights were still rather short, but as time went on, the risk from working parties increased, and we felt we could wait no longer.

The great day dawned with a cheerful wind and a glorious rain.

'If only this keeps on, we shall be OK tonight,' I exclaimed to Gerrie as we squelched along the muddy road to Hiltrup, the rain hissing about our ears and stinging our faces.

The night fulfilled our hopes. It was at about 5 o'clock in the afternoon that we presented ourselves at the camp gate, laden with books, which we fervently prayed might hide the bulkiness of our persons.

We were both of the lean kind, and the knobs and protuberances that seemed to our excited imaginations to stick out like the Swiss Alps all over us were possibly not very noticeable.

Managing, despite fast-beating pulses, to maintain a casual manner, we informed the guard at the gate that we wanted to see our friends in the *Lazarett*.

To our surprise and consternation, he flatly refused the request, and no amount of argument or persuasion would budge him. We had almost despaired, when we saw a German NCO approaching, and we appealed to him. We had been admitted to the hospital before, we said. There had been no difficulty then. Why should we be prevented now?

The NCO was puzzled. Our manner evidently carried assurance, but his duty made him cautious. 'You must have a pass. You must get it in writing,' he said.

'We have no time now; our friends are very ill, one of them is dying,' we pleaded. 'It may be too late tomorrow.'

The sergeant relented. He made a sign to the guard, who stepped back as we advanced.

We passed through the main gate and entered the gate of the *Lazarett* enclosure. The first stage of our escape was accomplished. The great adventure lay ahead!

Our plan was to remain in the *Lazerett* until nearly eight o'clock, risking being searched for at roll call, because the maximum of darkness was necessary for our attempt.

At eight o'clock by our calculations, the great arc lamps would be lit and escape become impossible. So our dash up and over the barbed-wire barrier must be made five minutes before eight.

All went well. The hospital patients, now informed of our plans, reacted in different ways. One or two were enthusiastic. Some, however, were afraid – afraid for us, afraid of what would happen should they be held accomplices. But all were ready to stand by us loyally and see us through.

We had outstayed our time long before eight o'clock, but the guard had been changed without search being made for us, and our comrades kept us informed of the approach of any German, so that we were able to hide under the beds.

Cleeton fulfilled his promise, and at 7.30 we had the satisfaction of seeing him bring the massive dog into the ward.

At 7.40pm we shook hands with one or two. A handclasp, a muttered 'Good luck' and we were at the door of the hospital. It was dusk. The sentry seemed to be at the far end of the building.

We intended to dodge round a corner, risking the other sentry's vigilance, and make a dash for the particular portion of the fence noted on previous reconnaissances.

We were ready. All was well. Now! Suddenly the whole scene was illuminated. It was as light as day. The electric lights had been put on five minutes earlier than usual.

What was to be done? It seemed madness now to think of escape.

Our pals, clustering within the doorway, gasped. We must give it up. Postpone it. But that seemed equally hopeless, for our long visit to the *Lazarett* and absence from roll call must create suspicion on our return. Then, too, we were keyed up to the attempt.

In less time than it takes to tell, our minds were made up. We would chance it. The back of the sentry was towards us. We made a swift and silent dash along the building and round the corner. The other sentry was evidently round the next corner, but our attempt was over-looked by the windows of a German officers' room. For all we knew, a German might now be looking out.

We saw the diagonal post. According to agreement, previously decided by a toss-up, Burk went first. I watched him run up the cross-bar and seize the top wire. I waited in an agony of suspense. How slow

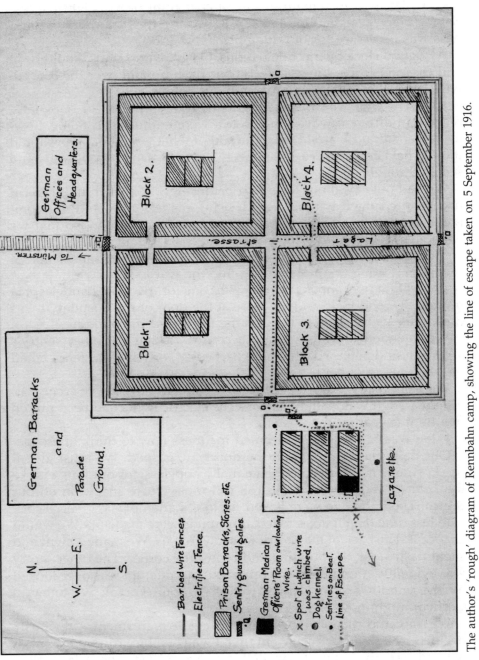

The author's 'rough' diagram of Rennbahn camp, showing the line of escape taken on 5 September 1916.

he seemed! Perhaps a rifle was pointing at my back from the window of the officers' mess. Surely I heard the sentry coming round the corner.

Every second seemed an hour. I could wait no longer. Gerrie was still on the cross-bar, and I made one dash at the fence to the left of him. I leapt and dragged myself up the tangle of barbed wire.

My jacket and fingers stuck on the barbs. I struggled miserably. I was on top, but hopelessly entangled. Desperately I dragged and wriggled. Gerrie was over; he was running down the slope. I writhed impotently, a splendid target for any sentry in the blaze of electric light. It cannot have been long, but it seemed an eternity – that horrible position. And then I got chest and body free and hurled myself head foremost over and downwards, tearing my clothing to ribbons and lacerating my fingers horribly.

I scrambled to my feet, panting and well-nigh exhausted, and stumbled down the grassy incline away from the dazzling lights.

Gasping, I fled after the dim shadow that was my companion.

He was making for a little spinney and I followed him. There we threw ourselves down, in the friendly shelter of the dark bushes to regain our breath.

The lights of Münster twinkled from the darkness a mile away; the nearer light of the camp shone down the track we had come. There was no noise, no sound of a rifle or cry of alarm.

We peered at each other in the darkness. We were free!

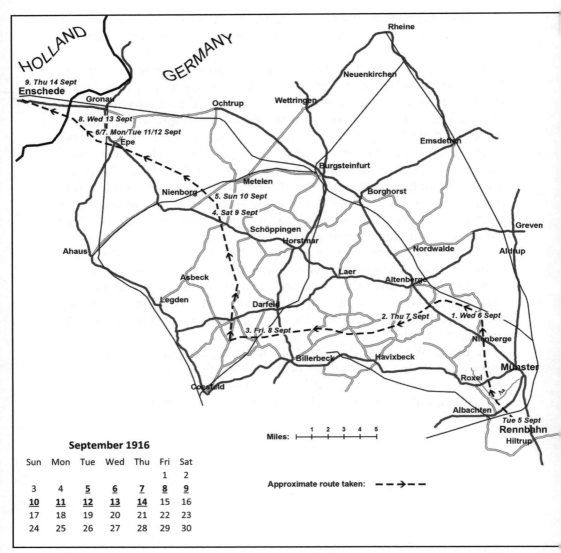

Approximate route taken: - - - ➤ - -

The escapees left Rennbahn on the evening of 5 September and reached Holland on the morning of 14 September. They travelled by night (between the hours of 10.00pm and 4.00am to avoid the risk of being seen) and hid by day, making a nine-night journey over ten calendar days. Many hours were lost in 'fruitless wanderings', and they often strayed off course. The above map gives an approximation, in the route taken and especially in the locations (indicated by day/date) where the escapees concealed themselves and rested during daylight hours. It has been created by reference to the route marked out by the author on a large-scale 1916 British War Office map of the Münster area, as well as by reference to this memoir.

Chapter 13

Escape Day One:
5–6 September (Tue/Wed)

Free! Even now we could hardly realise that we were out of the camp – unguarded, that apparently our absence at roll call had passed unnoticed, due probably to the resource and wit of one of our loyal friends.

It seemed incredible that our dash for the wire had been neither heard nor seen, with sentries only a few yards away.

We blessed the weather – the sort that tempts a sentry to turn up his coat collar and shut his eyes. It was raining heavily and had circumstances been other than they were, we should have thought our own position anything but enviable, for we were beneath a dripping hedge, lying among sodden leaves and wet grass.

As it was, we lay there, glad to rest, for since no alarm had been raised, we concluded that we were safest where we were until later.

We had previously decided that it would not be safe to walk except between 10.00pm and 4.00am as our route lay through farming areas for the greater part, where the inhabitants rose very early and where the sight of strange men, without great-coats and in prison uniform, would cause an alarm that would set all the dogs and men in the neighbourhood on our track.

So we bound up our bleeding hands, did what we could to pin our torn clothing into some semblance of usefulness and decency, and refreshed ourselves from our bottle of alcohol and crème de menthe.

Not till then did we really take stock of our position. True we were free, but there are degrees of freedom and our newly-gained liberty was a very precarious affair, which might terminate suddenly and ignominiously.

But it was not wise to dwell on such possibilities. The hour was growing late. We held a brief council of war and crawling from under our wet shelter, we cautiously rose to our feet and struck out together in what we thought to be the direction we had previously decided on.

This was one which kept in view, at a distance, the main railway line leading to Holland.

The darkness, however, made it impossible to take any bearings and suddenly there loomed up what was evidently the railway embankment of some branch line. We did not like crossing this but decided to risk it, and we crawled on hands and knees across a turnip field which bordered it, and, scrambling up the slope, glanced along the metals.

There, not fifty yards away, stood a signal box. As we watched, lights glimmered and moved. We must make a dash for it. We sprang across the lines and plunged down the other side. I heard a muttered curse from my comrade and a heavy thud, and the next moment I was flung headlong, striking the cindery path heavily as I fell. We had been tripped up by a stretch of signal wires, which sang in a most astonishing manner and threatened to give an alarm to the whole German railway system. Silently cursing our carelessness, we made a leap up what appeared to be another slope.

With a crash and a clatter, Hell's furies seemed to break loose. We had landed in the midst of some sort of dump for tins and cans, and the row we raised was terrific.

Tins flew in all directions as we floundered over. We sweated with fear, but we did not stay to await the result of our blunder. The lights in the cabin flashed, and we ran into the darkness beyond.

We found ourselves in a ploughed field, whose heavy wet sods seemed to cling to our feet as though determined to hold us back. Presently, however, we were among standing corn and pushing through this we came to another hedge. We seemed to be drawing near to some building, but it was impossible to see far in the darkness, and our surmise was only made certainty when we found ourselves in an orchard adjoining a small garden.

We had a vague idea of our position as we could still see the lights of Münster behind us, and other lights told us we were not far from two other prison camps. Indeed, we passed between these two camps, in one of which I knew lay a friend, Ossie Frost – sleeping, I hoped, peacefully. I wondered what he would say if he could see us now.

Suddenly from the darkness a dog barked. We jumped as though we had been shot. We were far too near a farm for our peace of mind, and we struck off at an angle till the barking died away. Evidently some watchdog, chained to his kennel, had detected the presence of prowlers.

It was then that a new noise reached us – the rush of water immediately in front of us. This must be the river marked on our maps, which we knew we must cross and which we expected to find a small stream. Recent rains, however, had swelled it into a very considerable flood, which it seemed dangerous to attempt to cross.

We wasted a valuable hour in a search for a bridge, not daring to separate lest one might mistake a stranger for his companion on the return journey along the bank. Finally, there being no help for it, we plunged into the river and tripping and floundering over the loose stones of its bed, we half waded and half swam across.

By now we had lost sight of the lights of Münster, and for the rest of that night we continued our journey without taking any rest and without further adventures, until the paling of the eastern sky warned us of the approach of dawn. It was time we sought a hiding place for the day, and as the gathering light showed a big wood ahead, we made for its cover.

There was a village not very far away from it, but we were too tired to proceed further, and so we contented ourselves with what shelter it afforded, which was poor enough, as we discovered later.

At the time, however, we were too exhausted to weigh up chances of safety and discovery, and we were a sorry spectacle, with clothing torn further by our scrambling progress and hands and faces dirty and scratched. Our chief fears were for our precious and scanty provisions, which we expected to find sodden and spoilt.

We were ravenous, but we knew that we must be exceedingly careful with our rations, and already we realised that our progress could not be as speedy and direct as had seemed possible when we planned the adventure.

Fortunately, what provisions we had were well protected either in small tins or waterproof cloth, and our precious maps and compasses, together with a number of prison photographs, which I had determined to smuggle out of the country, were in a small mackintosh case next to the skin [many of these smuggled photographs can be seen in this book].

Biscuits and provender, when wet at all, dried on us again. As we lay under the shelter of undergrowth, we made our first meal – a French army biscuit and a bar of chocolate – and consulted our maps. So far we had not done badly, having maintained our direction roughly towards the frontier. We were not far from the railway line, which we intended, when possible, to keep in sight, and allowing for the detour it had been necessary to make to avoid Münster, we had accomplished some seven or eight miles towards our objective.

But we were cold and shivering; our clothing was wet through; our teeth chattered, and there seemed very little chance of our getting dry, as the morning was cold and grey. As the day advanced, however, the sun broke through and our hiding place became the centre of a little patch of warm sunlight. I felt immeasurably cheered and prepared to make myself as comfortable as possible. But Burk was uneasy; he was inclined to caution, and his knowledge of the backwoods of Canada told him that our shelter was not sufficient.

A low ditch lay behind us, and my companion pointed out that there we could lie covered by leaves and bracken, absolutely out of sight.

But the prospect of changing from my sunny spot to one among dank grasses and acute discomfort did not appeal to me at all, and I resisted his cautious council. While in the midst of our whispered argument, we heard the sharp crackle of a stick trodden underfoot.

We lay still, hardly daring to breathe, our bodies pressed to the ground beneath the thicket, our eyes staring through its thorny tangle. And this is what we saw. Coming towards us from the direction of the village were two sportsmen. They carried rifles and, worse than all, dogs were at their heels – dogs which every now and then sniffed and trotted a few yards into the undergrowth.

The men were talking to each other and making straight towards our hiding place. I could hear my heart pounding like a dynamo, and it seemed that the dogs must hear it too.

We gave ourselves up for lost, for if the men should see us, we had no chance against their loaded guns.

Visions of being marched back to camp, bedraggled and forlorn, assailed me in that moment. The men had approached to within a few feet of our position, yet they had noticed nothing unusual. Their path would lead them past our hiding place. It was the dogs that we had to fear.

Suddenly one of the animals pointed. It seemed to me that the brute saw us, for he looked straight at our bush. Then he lowered his head and trotted towards us nose down.

A kind of nausea overcame me. I closed my eyes and waited for the inevitable.

I remember hearing a sharp exclamation in German, and after what seemed an intolerable age, I opened my eyes. I could scarcely credit my own sight, for the two men had passed us by and were receding down the path, their dogs trotting quietly behind them.

My companion lay a little behind me, and as I slowly turned and looked at him, I saw beads of perspiration on his brow, and his strained eyes stared in a dazed manner out of his white, scratched face.

I realised that I must present a similar spectacle, and for a moment, a wild desire to laugh assailed me. The fact that we had been within an ace of discovery seemed, in my overwrought condition, indescribably funny, now that the tension was relaxed.

'What happened? I shut my eyes,' I whispered to Burk.

'The fellow seemed to call the dog to heel,' he answered, adding hurriedly: 'We had better get out of this. God knows they may be back any moment.'

Making sure that there was no one within sight, we scrambled out of the first hiding place and made for the low damp-looking ditch which Burk had first advocated. It was partly covered by low bushes and quite filled with dead leaves and loose bracken fronds.

We burrowed down into this wet mess, which, however uncomfortable it might be, at any rate afforded us complete cover, while enabling us to get some view of our surroundings.

And well it was that we effected the exchange when we did, for distant shots in the wood told us that the sportsmen were busy finding smaller game. Our day in that accursed wood was one long series of alarms.

No sooner had the shots ceased than voices took their place. The whole nearby village seemed to have gone on holiday and chosen this wood as a picnic place. People passed at intervals along the track taken by the sportsmen, and the shouts of children playing were all around us. Once, indeed, several youngsters invaded the brambles under which we had been hiding so short a time ago, obviously on the hunt for early blackberries.

Weary as we were, it was quite impossible to sleep at all, and when, towards five o'clock, the children took themselves off home and the wood became quiet, we were glad to scramble out from our sodden bed and sit for a short time risking discovery in the last rays of the setting sun.

Chapter 14

Escape Day Two:
6–7 September (Wed/Thu)

We ventured to the edge of the wood in order to get our bearings and could make out, a mile or so away, the railway line which we meant to follow.

Accordingly, when darkness set in, we started, after a consultation over the illuminated compass we carried and another meal of French army biscuit and chocolate. The fields were deserted, and soon we were close to the track.

How swiftly we might be carried to liberty if only we were travelling by train! The thought was too much for Gerrie Burk. Such easy means of locomotion should surely be put to use.

He suggested that we should board a train in motion, as he told me he had done once or twice in Canada, and pointed out a sharp bend ahead of us, on which the engine might possibly slow down.

I was very averse to such a proceeding, for, I urged, it was too dangerous – at any rate, for one inexperienced as myself – and I had no wish to be smashed up by a foolhardy venture of such a nature. But I followed Burk towards the spot he indicated and lay beside him close to the rails, ready to follow his lead if the thing proved easy.

We waited for about three-quarters of an hour and then there came the distant rumble of an approaching train. I felt more like a prospective suicide than a dashing reckless 'hobo' (train jumper). The headlights of the oncoming train nearly blinded me as I raised my head and waited for it to slow down somewhat.

But (and I must confess, to my immense relief) the train did not slow down in the least, and in a flash it was past, giving us a brief vision of comfortable travel and leaving us foolishly agape at its receding rear lights.

After that there was no more talk of boarding trains. To tackle a Canadian locomotive was one thing. To board a train of whose construction we knew nothing, in an enemy country on a dark night, was another.

So, we decided to keep to the fields, which ran parallel to the track, and this we did for some time until we were utterly tired of scrambling over hedges. Never have I seen such tiny fields as those bordering that railway line. We had no sooner scrambled and broken our way through one obstacle than it seemed we were confronted with another. There were hedges everywhere, and the country seemed thickly dotted with small farms.

Constantly, our approach was the signal for a loud outburst of barking. Sometimes we got near enough to hear the rattle of a chain as a watch-dog sprang frantically up and down in his efforts to be free to give chase.

Germany seemed a land of dogs that night, all anxious to put an end to our journey, and we soon decided that it was madness to court disaster by any further progress so near to the line.

We therefore broke away at right angles and floundered about making what headway we could. By now we were tired out, and the strain of our months of captivity and the excitement of recent adventures were beginning to tell on our bodies and tempers.

We felt the need of sleep, yet we realised that if we were to spend the hours of darkness in resting, at our present rate of progress we would never make the frontier in anything like the calculated time.

At one point we were startled by sounds from the other side of a hedge. We lowered ourselves into the ditch, thinking perhaps that poachers were afield. The sounds grew nearer, and we prepared to put up a fight under cover of darkness should we be discovered. Suddenly a head was raised above the hedge, and we dimly made out the pricked ears and long white nose of a horse!

We must have staggered on for another hour, and if anyone has tried the experiment of a cross-country walk over unknown ground on a dark night, he will understand something of the feeling of helplessness we had. Our knowledge of the use of a compass was limited. The stars seemed a better guide, but they were frequently hidden by misty clouds and afforded us little help.

When the first hint of day appeared, we gave up the struggle, and, warned by the danger of our former resting-place, we set about looking for a place where we could lie entirely concealed.

The light was too dim to see far, but we found a very fine hedge bordering a field of stacked oats. Long branches with yellowing leaves stretched out from the hedge across a broad deep ditch, and this we decided would make a splendid hiding place.

With the craft of a woodsman, Burk cut branches from the underpart of the hedge, in such a way that their absence would be unnoticed should anyone pass by. Then we pulled bundles of oats into the ditch, which held a quantity of water, gathered other branches and rotting material, and, lying down, pulled them over ourselves.

We were, we felt sure, completely hidden, and glad to stretch our weary limbs, we hoped fervently for sleep. But sleep was long in coming, for the oats, pressed down by our weight, soon became sodden by the water below, and from the patter-patter on the leaves above us, we knew that it was raining.

However, sleep we did for a time, and woke with sensations of acute discomfort, for our ditch was more like a choked stream than ever, though the rain had evidently ceased since the pattering above us had stopped.

But if I heard no sound of rain, I did hear other sounds and these only too clearly. There was the rattle of a machine, a distant 'swish, swish' and, what was worse, the sound of several voices.

I would have liked to have scrambled out and made a dash for it, for the prospect of another day of nerve strain, alarm, and most probable capture in this pneumonia-bed of a ditch was not exactly a bright one.

A slight rustle beside told me that Gerrie was awake, but I dared not speak to him and lay straining my ears for the sounds from the field.

The regular rattle of the machine told us that reaping was in progress on the far side of the field, but there were voices much nearer and a sound as of raking between the stooks of oats. Would the missing sheaves be noticed should carting begin? Were there any accursed dogs nosing about?

I would have given worlds to turn over and lie on the other side, so cramped was my arm, but I feared lest the least movement of our covering should betray us, though the spreading branches above us should have hidden any such action.

Towards what was probably midday, we heard children's voices, and a new fear assailed us.

We had seen the day before how these youngsters loved to poke about in bushes and hedges, and now we dreaded their happy shouts more than any other sounds.

Shortly after this it seemed that a party of workers, men and women, were resting near to us for their midday meal. The clatter of the machine stopped; the words of the labourers, had we been good

German scholars, would have been perfectly clear to us. As it was we distinctly heard the words '*Zwei Engländer*' (two Englishmen) repeated several times.

We were at once a prey to the gravest fears. Had we been noticed? Did a protruding foot or fluttering rag betray us?

'Two Englishmen.' There it was again.

Surely they would not sit there munching their rye bread if they really suspected that within ten yards lay two escaped prisoners of war! News of our flight must naturally have been broadcast; the frontier guards would be ready for us, and our escape be the theme of conversation all along our suspected route. Perhaps it was under discussion now. I hoped that the repetition of '*Zwei Engländer*' meant nothing worse.

Ah, how hungry we were! There were these fat Germans (for so we pictured them) enjoying their dinners so near to us, while we lay with empty bellies in a poisonous wet ditch.

Then we heard children running nearby. They were evidently having a game of 'tig' or a race round the field, for their flying feet passed so close to us that an outstretched hand might have grabbed one by the leg.

'What was that?' The patter-patter of rain! Now surely work would stop and our danger be over. And indeed it seemed that this was so – for a time. But we dared not move, not knowing to what distance the reapers had gone. The rain (which had seemed blessed for once) soon stopped and work was renewed. It appeared now from the rumble of wheels that a cart was in the field and coming straight in our direction. Surely we could not fail to be discovered? The missing sheaves would be noticed and suspicions aroused.

The children were coming again. There was a rustle of the hedge some yards away. What the hell was happening now? I felt a weight on my leg; the branches above me moved. I had a glimpse of a blue worsted stocking and a bare knee. A boy was actually standing upon me, stretching up to the hedge above. I should move; I MUST move – and then?

But suddenly the lad sprang away and joined his companions further along the hedge. I lay still, blessing Burk and his wood-craft and the caution that had preserved our liberty, if not our lives.

That was the last alarm we had that day. As evening fell, we heard the workers depart, and we waited a long time before we dared move or even speak.

Chapter 15

Escape Day Three:
7–8 September (Thu/Fri)

When we raised ourselves, it was to find the field deserted, most of the stooks gone, and the grain on the far side all cut. There was no sign of farm buildings, though a winding track through two fields and round the bend of a small wood made us suspect that these were only hidden from us by the trees. We peered cautiously about, and seeing that there were no cows or other grazing cattle in the adjoining fields, we drew ourselves stiffly from the ditch and sat under the hedge branches; for surely, we thought, no one could have any further business there that evening.

We were so cold that our numbed fingers could scarcely fumble for the tobacco we so longed to sample. But we did drag it out at last and even succeeded in finding a dry match after endless strikings.

It was a work of patience to get those pipes alight, but when we did so, ah! – then, never did 'the fragrant weed' seem so good.

We tried to warm our fingers on the bowls of our pipes, and when we had enjoyed them to the full, we pulled out our fodder, the usual army biscuit, very much the worse for wear, and spread it with slices of Oxo cubes.

The inner man refreshed, if but scantily, we next rummaged for our precious maps and compasses and sat under our hedge planning the night's journey.

My compass had proved of little use. The illuminated dial of Burk's was invaluable to us, and by its use we hoped, now that we were becoming used to night walking, to make a more direct progress north-west towards the Dutch frontier town of Enschede.

I pulled out my little diary and made a few entries with a stub of a pencil, adding under that for 7 September: 'Oat bed. Hell-of-a-day.'

Gerrie Burk dozed off again, and I relit my pipe and sat musing upon our extraordinary good fortune so far, until darkness closed down and the time came for us to resume our journey.

We had decided that we were some miles west of the town of Altenberge, which was itself a good deal to the west of our intended route, and being so far out of our direction, we planned to continue over what should prove a more direct, if less desolate area. When we set out, we realised that we were to have a little light from a waxing moon, and though this made our going easier, it also added to the risks of discovery.

Hedges still seemed abundant, but we made good going for some time, till we considered it necessary to take another compass bearing. What was our consternation to find that the precious illuminated instrument which Burk had carried was missing? He sought frantically in all his numerous pockets but could not find it.

A kind of dull rage possessed me at this carelessness, as I deemed it, and I said curtly enough: 'We'll just have to go back and chance using the flash-lamp to find the damned thing.'

And indeed that seemed the only thing to do, for the thought of losing such a precious item of equipment was not to be harboured at all. So back we went with but very little hope really, trying to locate the exact places where we had broken through the hedges, for there, if anywhere, we had a chance of recovering our loss. Our hearts felt heavy, and we could not trust ourselves to speak. The gaps in the hedges we did manage by use of the flash-lamp to find, but not the compass, and we must have spent an hour in fruitless search, when at the tallest and most difficult hedge Burk gave a triumphant gasp. There, faintly gleaming lay the compass! We hurried to retrace our steps once more and make up for lost time.

Whether nervousness or fatigue made us blunder, I do not know, but after a couple of hours' steady tramp, doubts began to overwhelm me. We did not seem to be passing such landmarks as we had expected to meet with.

Within five miles, I had calculated, we ought to cross a railway line, but we must have gone almost twice that distance, and still no sign of a railway appeared.

I halted irresolute, and Burk came to a standstill. 'What is it?' he asked.

'We're wrong somehow,' I muttered and pulled out map, compass, and flash lamp. We sat down in the middle of a field, without more ado, and using the light, I explained why I thought we must be off our route. 'We should have crossed that line long ago,' I said. 'We must be too far south-west.'

At first my companion was incredulous, and then, realising that we were indeed miles out of our way and hopelessly lost, he broke into a torrent of abuse.

'You ******* fool, you!' he shouted, forgetting caution in his anger and excitement and rising to his feet.

'Why the ******* hell have you got us into this mess? I left the route to you; it was your blasted job.'

Days and nights of anxiety and frayed nerves had prepared the way for this. I jumped to my feet, scattering map, compass and flash lamp.

'You damned swine!' I shouted. 'Who are you to talk? What about the compass?' My words poured forth as freely as Burk's. We glared at one another furiously.

I saw fists clenched; he stepped forward menacingly. I raised my own as his arm shot out.

It was then I saw the light!

One moment I was a savage animal, anxious to knock my companion senseless and have done with him, and the next I had seized his outflung arm by the wrist and twisted him round, so that he too saw the approaching light.

Almost with the same action, I dragged him with me as I fell flat on my face; and there we lay, just raising our heads a little to stare at the oncoming danger which threatened us both.

Our anger vanished in a flash; our quarrel was forgotten in this extremity which needed our combined thought and action.

The moon had become obscured by clouds, and the light we had both seen appeared to be coming directly across the field towards us. Suddenly another followed it, and another.

This must be an organised search such as we had feared all along. Should we move, or would the lights flash upon us if we did so? We could not decide. Our emotions of the last few minutes seemed to have paralysed us.

The moon might sail out from behind her clouds at any moment now and betray us, for we lay quite exposed on flat ground.

It struck me as curious that the lights kept such a direct line, and yet the bearers of them did not call to one another. Suddenly the first light switched to the left; another moment and the second did likewise. One more period of uncertainty and the third had followed the others. Then the moon emerged, and we saw clearly enough what had happened.

We lay in such a position that our eyes were directed towards the bend of a narrow road, and the lights which we had seen had been those of three bicycles. There was no hedge or fence of any description to break the oncoming lights, and the cyclists had simply followed one another round the bend and were now out of sight.

We raised ourselves and looked at each other sheepishly, realising, without putting it into words, what a serious break this false alarm had prevented. And only just in time, for – keyed to the pitch we had both been, with tempers on edge, and nerves frayed – it might have been murder once we came to blows.

My imagination pictured for a moment the possible outcome of our quarrel had fate not intervened.

I was the taller by a head and, moreover, Burk was suffering from a weak heart, developed in captivity and naturally aggravated by recent events. What use would freedom have been to me, even supposing I could have won it alone, if I had, in a fit of temper, killed so fine a comrade!

Silently we got to our feet and, picking up our scattered belongings, turned our attention to the map as though nothing had happened.

We must bear to the north and hope to strike some means of checking our position. So far we had avoided all main roads, though we knew that sooner or later we must strike them at right angles and most certainly we must cross the railway line somewhere.

Meanwhile, we felt the pangs of hunger. We were sick of the everlasting French army biscuits and chocolate, and what we had of them was rapidly dwindling to a very small ration. It was the time of the apple harvest. If we could find a well-laden orchard, the fruit would be a welcome change and perhaps prevent skin trouble, which threatened to develop through our dry salty diet.

With this idea in mind, instead of avoiding the next farm we saw, we made deliberately towards it and approached from the side which seemed to be sheltered by trees. No sooner had we got within a stone's throw of the surrounding wall, however, than the usual clamour began. Loud and frantic barking woke the echoes, but despite this hullaballoo, we swung ourselves over the wall and down between the laden branches.

For the next five minutes, we threw caution to the winds. A spirit of recklessness and schoolboy adventure must have possessed us, for we carried on as though no dog were straining to get at us. Burk was up a tree in a moment, filling his pockets and shaking the branches, while I stuffed as many apples as I could find on the ground into my pockets. The main farm building was hidden from us by trees, and we did not know whether the family was roused and about to burst out upon us or not.

I cannot remember giving the matter much thought. The most important thing in life just then seemed to be to secure as many apples as possible and make a bolt for it. And this we did and ran, chuckling with glee, until we were out of earshot. Then, finding a convenient hedge, we sat down and surveyed our spoil.

Those ripe, juicy apples were ambrosia; and well laden with a future supply, we trudged on until at last we made out the raised telegraph posts and twinkling lights that denoted the long-expected railway line.

We approached as cautiously as the moonlight permitted, in little spurts, under cover of temporary darkness, and made for a spot well away from the signal lights, where nothing seemed to break the monotony of the line.

This time we did not blunder over any wires or dumps of refuse tins. Once across, we kept in the shadow of a tall hedge until we had crossed a couple of fields and the railway was well behind us.

For the rest of the night we plodded on without further excitement other than the occasional barking of dogs as we skirted farm buildings.

We lost ourselves frequently and wandered about 'going west by north' – and, to misquote Kipling, 'eating apples all the way and throwing the cores about.'

Towards morning (8 September), we approached a small wood, and as it seemed in the midst of desolate country, we decided to camp there for the day. Our chief difficulty was our lack of water, for having left the farm lands behind, we seemed to be in an absolutely dry and barren area. We had a little of the precious liquid, however, in the army water-bottle, which had been pushed into my hands by Jack Billson. Since we were so far from road or habitation, we decided to make a small fire, sufficiently large to boil a bully-beef stew.

With tiny twigs and straws, which we cut with a pen-knife, we kept a small flame going in the lid of the beef tin. We dared not risk a larger one, and while Burk fed the fire, I cut up half the bully beef into small cubes and poured the remainder of our water on to them.

It was a ticklish business and a long one, boiling that stew, for the tin had to be supported by short branches, which were continually catching fire. We 'thickened the gravy' with three Oxo cubes.

We devoured this 'effervescing saline' – though had we been less famished than we were, we could not have touched the stuff – and after treading out and raking over our little fire, we lay down under a hedge and prepared for a good sleep. We were dry and we were fed. Moreover, we were dog tired and assured that we were safe where we were.

Hardly had we lain down, however, than a low hum reached our ears. We lay listening and wondering. Were we, after all, nearer a road than we thought? The direction of the sound seemed to change and its tone to alter. There was no mistaking that drone.

It was not the engine of any car but that of an aeroplane. We could tell that the machine was low down. What could it be doing in such an out-of-the-way place at such an hour, for it was now just becoming really light? What indeed but searching for something or someone? We looked at each other and our eyes asked the same question. Then, making sure we were well hidden, we waited till the machine glided into view above the tree tops. It was a small plane, and it crossed our wood and flew low over some moorland to the west. We watched it go with relief and then, to our consternation, it turned and made again towards our hiding place.

We thanked our lucky stars that we had made so small a fire, for we now felt convinced that search was being made for us by aeroplane. As it was, we were hidden from view, but this new danger made us very uneasy. The machine was now overhead. It passed a little way to the east, turned south, and circled twice before heading away in that direction.

I think that had we been allowed to drop off to sleep straight away, nothing would have roused us for hours except an earthquake; but now made restless by this unwelcome visitor, we became conscious of an intolerable thirst. Our mouths felt dry and parched and unbearably salty. We wished we had not eaten all our apples on the march and turned from side to side restlessly. When we did sleep, it was but fitfully and uneasily. From time to time one or the other of us rose and made a short journey in search of water – always in vain.

So passed the day of 8 September. We had been three nights on the march and had not accomplished half our journey. We could hardly hope now to reach the frontier in less than a week.

Chapter 16

Escape Day Four:
8–9 September (Fri/Sat)

Towards evening we decided to set off earlier than usual, in the hope of finding water and of seeing some means of learning our direction more precisely. The country for some miles seemed to be moorland, which had evidently had no rain for some time, and there was no sign of human habitation.

We came at last, however, within sight of a road leading northwards, but we dared not approach it until darkness had fallen. So we rested for a time where we were, but soon realised that there was to be no darkness, as a clear moon sailed into the sky.

Burk was very averse to road travel, and only the need of correcting our position could have persuaded him to leave the open country. This proved to be very little better than a cart track and, though we saw no signpost, we did see, standing near a small farm, an old-fashioned pump.

Our water-bottles were dry, and our mouths burned with thirst. Regardless of everything else, Burk seized the pump handle and pumped vigorously. The pump emitted groans and shrieks in plenty, but no water. We tried to prime it from a dirty muddy mess in the trough below, but after a few more eldritch wails, the thing stopped and refused to function at all.

Suddenly, we heard a window shoot open in the building nearby, and we bolted into the fields behind and did not stop running until we saw something slowly moving in the next field. To our surprise it was a solitary cow, and the sight of it there, silhouetted against the sky, was so unexpected that we pulled up simultaneously.

If it had suddenly jumped over the moon and proved to be that fascinating animal of nursery days, I do not think we could have been any more astonished than we were.

'Can you milk?' asked Gerrie. 'No,' I replied promptly. 'Well, I can,' he returned and, hastily gathering a handful of grass, he advanced towards the creature somewhat in the same manner as a photographer approaching some rare species of bird which might take flight at any moment.

I followed his example, and we closed in upon the unsuspecting cow to within a few feet. Then we offered our oblations humbly, making what we thought to be conciliatory noises suitable to the occasion.

She was pleased to accept my offering and allowed me to stroke her forehead gently and then hold her head. Burk meanwhile was out of view to me, presumably doing wonders somewhere on his knees with the cow and his water-bottle, though there seemed to me a more steady stream of language than of milk. The cow shifted uneasily. I heard a very loud 'Damn!' from my friend and realised that he had dropped the bottle. With that he whipped off his headgear, a Belgian forage cap, and did his best to use that as a pail.

But by this time the cow had had enough. With an indignant snort and a whisk of her tail, she broke away and trotted off, leaving us with a very bad impression of German cows in general.

Burk's language was equal to the occasion, if his milking powers were not.

We next tried to get a drink from a small and very stagnant pool. It was overgrown with slimy scum and stank abominably, but we were so terribly thirsty that we were ready for anything and knelt down to drink. Once the beastly stuff was in our mouth, however, caution prevailed, and we did nothing more than rinse it round and spit it out again. However, poisonous as it tasted, it did seem to rid our mouths of the dry salty flavour that had tortured us, and kept us going till, to our great joy, we came upon a small stream of clear water. In this we fairly wallowed, drinking and bathing our faces. Then we filled our water-bottles, ate a little of our dwindling food, and took a small sip each of our crude alcohol before setting out again.

Still we were more or less lost, and did not know on what part of the map our track lay. The sight of a road, leading, as we thought, due north was a great relief, and my instinct was to get on to it at once and risk the danger in order to find a signpost.

Burk, however, disagreed, and we had an argument which threatened to become a second quarrel, until he agreed to accompany me at some distance behind.

We had arranged, before we made an attempt to escape, that should discovery threaten one, the other should make a bolt for it, and let no false sense of loyalty cause an unnecessary end to his success. Accordingly, since I insisted on the road, I took the risk and walked on boldly, followed some thirty yards behind by Burk.

Sure enough, we had not gone more than half a mile before I saw a signpost at a crossroads. I could see no one about, and approaching it carefully, I made out the names of Schappingham [? probably Schöppingen] on one side and Asbeck and Darfeld on the other.

These I located on the map and found we were much further south than we wanted to be. I was not satisfied. We had heard rumours in camp of names being altered to mislead fugitives near the frontier, and although it now seems hardly a likely procedure, at this time I was distrustful and determined to push on along the road, which at any rate seemed to promise good progress in the right direction.

Accordingly we continued as before, and after the rough cross-country scrambling that we had been used to, this seemed a delightfully easy advance.

I began to forget the danger in the enjoyment of the road, which led through some fine woodland, looking very beautiful in the moonlight; and I grew careless.

Consequently, on seeing a line of poplars which denoted another cross road, I did not proceed with our accustomed caution, but hurried forward, after a glance back to see that Gerrie was following, in order to read the signpost.

I saw the cross road and the signpost, but what I did not see, until it was too late, was the sentry box below the post.

One horrified glance took in this and a huge wagon at the side of the right-hand road. I heard the rattle of a chain and a fierce roaring bark, saw a uniformed figure step out and heard the challenge: '*Wer da?*' (Who goes there?).

I realised in a moment of acute dismay the disaster my carelessness had precipitated. In that moment I had turned and, with a flying leap, cleared the hedge behind me, before the guard had time to fire.

Dodging between two poplar trees, I ran in sheer terror. I heard shots ring out and wondered desperately if the dog were loosed on us. I thought I caught a glimpse for a moment of Burk's figure fleeing across the field further back, but my senses were confused.

I ran like a madman, weariness forgotten in the fear that impelled me. I remember bursting and crashing through hedges, leaping low obstacles, and never stopping till I thought I had shaken off possible pursuit. Then I threw myself flat and drew in great sobbing breaths on the cool grass.

My heart throbbed painfully, and I wondered about Burk – whether he were safe or whether my foolhardiness had led him into the trap. Then a memory of that other running figure returned to me, and I began to hope that we were not far apart. Rising, I crept along behind a hedge, peering through for any sight of my lost companion. I wandered about. I re-crossed a field, whistling softly, and calling his name.

I had begun to despair of our reunion, when, on poking my head through a low hedge, I saw a round object protruding from it some ten or a dozen yards away. It seemed to move slightly, and I was puzzled to know what it could be, in the fitful moonlight, which spread a haziness around things.

As I looked, the round object appeared to grow two legs beneath it, and I recognised the hindquarters of my pal, with a relief and pleasure inexpressible.

I realised that from his position I must present a similarly grotesque nether view, and we must have been a sight for the gods to laugh at, kneeling on opposite sides of that hedge each with a scared white face watching the contortions of two spindly half-naked legs.

But the gods being mirthful were likewise kind, and as we gripped hands, we had good reason to marvel at our escape and the strange manner of our meeting.

There was still need for great caution, and when we continued our march, it was far from the road, but parallel with it, for now we knew where we were. Our adventures at the crossroads, though nearly disastrous, had served one good purpose. It had confirmed the position of the first signpost, for our maps had shown the second set of roads to be where we had found them; and the fact that it was guarded by sentry box and patrol wagon strengthened our opinion that we were, at any rate, not more than twenty-five miles from the frontier.

We had been lost before and spent precious hours in fruitless wanderings, but at last, we thought, we could go forward sure of our direction, though with all the greater need for caution.

The moon was very bright, and the countryside looked very beautiful, for we were now in a well-wooded district.

Following the compass guiding, we plunged boldly into the woods; and to help our steps, and as a weapon of defence against dogs, we cut ourselves heavy staffs or cudgels four to five foot long.

Each night of that journey from Rennbahn had left some indelible memory, but this night, apart from the scare of the sentry, left impressions of sheer beauty.

The woods lay so quiet, so wonderfully peaceful in the moonlight. There was no wind to stir the branches, nor voice to wake the silence. In the more open spaces the shadows lay like velvet; and like velvet, too, was the carpet of pine needles and dead leaves underneath our feet.

Yet it was a ghostlike eerie beauty, for man is a creature of the daylight and does not often wander among strange places under the moon. We felt the romance of it, and somehow the danger and the risk added to the enjoyment of the experience. Tired as we were and beginning to feel more than tired – out of condition, almost ill – the night uplifted us, and the tall trees comforted.

Sometimes the going was difficult, thick underbrush had to be broken through at times, and when drifting clouds hid the moon, the forest grew bewildering.

The sound of our own progress, when it was necessary to force our way, seemed a rude disturbance of the quiet. Sometimes we stopped and listened, but when our movements were still, the night answered only with its silence.

We must have travelled through several miles of forest before we saw the edge of the wood. The tree trunks thinned, and as we reached their confines, we found ourselves looking down from a height upon the plain below. We could see a small village below us, with its roofs shining like silver under the moon's rays. A little stream ran through the village and dwindled to a silver thread in the dim distance.

With the aid of our staffs we scrambled down the rocky cliff. We thought we might pass through the village; it looked so locked in sleep. But in Germany one never seemed to approach a village or farm without rousing those lightest of sleepers, the dogs; and hearing one or two, we decided to make a detour.

This we did and had crossed several fields, approaching the hedges cautiously, when through one of them, we saw quite a broad road. It lay very white across our track, and we crouched behind the hedge, watching and listening for movement or sound. And it seemed that we heard a low murmur of voices, though we were not sure.

We listened for some time, but heard nothing, so we crawled as quietly as possible through a thin place and wriggled down into a ditch beside the road. We dared not cross that gleaming surface till we were quite sure that it was safe to do so, and as we crouched there we distinctly heard the sound of voices further along the road. We dared not go back. It was madness to go forward, so we lay down in the ditch and made ourselves as flat as possible.

I had a vague sense of something moving on the road towards us. The grasses above the ditch stirred and then parted, and I made out the shape of a great hound sniffing among the herbage.

I gripped my cudgel lightly but made no other movement, for some instinct warned me that our only chance of safety lay in absolute stillness. The beast drew nearer; it sniffed at Gerrie, and then I felt its warm breath on my face. Neither of us made a movement. The dog lifted its great head as though about to give tongue, and then, evidently thinking better of it, it sniffed at us again and trotted quietly away on to the road.

We had had a most marvellous escape, but we hardly dared to breathe yet. We did not know how soon the animal might come back or whether its master was approaching our refuge. We waited and heard no sound. All seemed deserted again. I whispered to Burk. We decided to cross the road a little lower down, where a few poplars cast their shadows across it; so we dragged ourselves along the ditch stealthily, and when we reached the shadow of the first tree, we wormed our way across the road eel fashion, hoping thus to be unnoticed should anyone be glancing from either direction.

Once across, we crawled through a fence on the other side and quickly put as big a distance as possible between ourselves and that road. We continued for some way through fields and pasture lands, avoiding the buildings, until a faint light in the east told us that it was dangerous to proceed further. Moreover, we were worn out and longed for a rest. The only shelter we could find was that of a hedge along a field.

It had wide-spreading branches and a ditch beneath, similar to that in which we had hidden by the oat-field. But it was necessary to find straw or something more than branches to act as bedding, and as we dared not delay longer, we threw our staffs and water-bottles under the hedge to mark the place and went to find material. It was none too safe a refuge, being obviously on farm land, but we dared not delay until the approach of dawn, for the German labourers seemed to rise before 4.00am, and we might not find a better place. I crossed the field with Burk, and we separated to gather some armfuls of corn and long grasses.

Carrying these before me, I was making my way back when, coming round a bend in the hedge some distance away, I made out two figures. I halted, irresolute. They were two farm girls carrying pails. They saw me, and I must have looked like some fantastic scarecrow, with arms and legs in flapping rags, a forage cap on my head, and a body of straw.

One of them dropped her pail with a startled exclamation, retrieved it hurriedly and darted back from whence she came, followed by her companion.

I dumped the stuff in our ditch and turned to meet Burk. Quickly, I explained the danger. 'We cannot stay here,' I said. 'They'll send someone else to see what's up. They may have taken me for a scarecrow, but scarecrows don't walk about and carry off corn for themselves.'

So we collected our belongings and made off for another mile or so. We became alarmed at the prospect of daylight breaking before we had discovered a suitable hiding place and, seeing a small coppice, we climbed the low wall on its nearest side. Here we found a deep ditch overgrown with shrubs running through its entire length, so we wormed our way down into it, pulling leaves and briars over the top of us.

We made a poor meal of biscuits and the remains of the bully beef and drank a little water from the water-bottle. Then, utterly worn out, we fell fast asleep.

Perhaps we slept one hour, perhaps two. Our rest was rudely disturbed, and we awoke once more to consciousness of immediate danger.

It seemed that we could not choose a secluded spot anywhere on our line of march. We had trudged half the night through quiet, lonely woods, and now, when it was time for our sorely-needed rest, we were in the midst of enemies again.

Though we could only see through our protecting screen for a distance of two or three yards' radius, the sounds we heard told us plainly enough that we were close to a farm. Indeed, we were in the little cluster of trees built to protect the house from the winds, and in the dim light of early dawn the building itself had never been observed, screened as it was in this way.

We could hear the lowing of cows and the rattle of pails in the byre, the shouts of a farm hand and the clucking of fowls.

Had it been dusk we would have tried to steal out unobserved and make off to another hiding place, but we knew that an appearance in daylight would be fatal to the success of our venture. So we had no choice, once more, but to lie still and hope for our luck to hold.

I felt desperately hungry again and very weak and would have given worlds for a drink of the good milk which I knew was being carried from the byre. We could hear the clatter of empty pails and the noise of full ones being set down on stone flags.

Our chief anxiety was lest one of the dogs, of which there were sure to be a few about the farm, should detect our presence and draw attention to our hiding place.

We managed, under our covering, to make a meal of chocolate and biscuit and assuaged further hunger by chewing gum, of which we each carried a little.

I was very sleepy, and in spite of our hazardous position, I was falling into a doze when I felt a pinch from Burk. Alert again in a moment, I listened. There was a rustling sound in the spinney. It was drawing nearer. 'Some damned dog,' I thought savagely, but remembering our recent adventure, I lay perfectly still. Rustle, rustle, went the leaves, a little nearer this time. We peered through the briars but could see nothing. Five minutes passed.

There it was again! This time the sound seemed to come from both sides of us, and above this slight noise we could hear the clop-clop of horses' feet on the stones or cobbles of the farmyard.

Suddenly something seemed to pounce! I broke into a sweat. Now we should know. There was a scuffle close to me, a frightened 'squawk', and I looked up into the fiercely red beady eye of a large black hen. She had something in her beak and was evidently the victor in some farmyard disagreement on the rights of property, as I could hear her disgruntled rival making off with angry clucks and scuffles.

All that excitement over a couple of hens! Well, we knew what the rustling sounds were now, and we did not anticipate any trouble from these members of the farmyard. And presently it began to rain, and we prayed that it might continue all day so that we might be left undisturbed; but towards midday the sun came out, and we heard children's voices about the farm. They seemed to be having rides on a wagon, probably to and from some harvest field, for we heard the squeak and rumble of heavily-laden carts at intervals.

Towards the close of the afternoon, just as we were beginning to feel almost secure, we heard the voices of several children close to the low wall that ran round the spinney. We had noticed from our retreat that one of the trees was an apple tree, and we now realised with great misgivings that the place was probably half an orchard.

We could hear someone scrambling over the wall. There were more shouts, and it was clear that quite a number of youngsters were within the area of trees.

What chance could we have now, in this tiny wood, of escaping discovery, if it was to be invaded by a horde of children? There was no time to take counsel. I felt the wisest plan was to lie still and trust that no one would think of rooting in a leaf-filled ditch and, should they do so, we must make a bolt for it, and hope to be out of sight before the children should set their elders on our track, though the chances were we would be seen by others working still in the fields.

There must have been at least five children in that place. Now and again we caught a glimpse of one or another of them. They were playing 'hide and seek', but fortunately they preferred less wet and uncomfortable hidey holes than ours and presumably sought the cover of tree trunks and bushes.

Presently, the game ceased. There was a shout from one of the children close at hand, and he came within our small range of view. Immediately the others clustered round, talking eagerly, and we saw that their attention was drawn to the apple tree that I have mentioned noticing.

Was this then the only apple tree in that wretched orchard? We were far too near to feel comfortable. Presently, the boy who had first appeared began to pull himself up into the branches. The others danced round excitedly.

He sat astride one of the branches and gave it a vigorous shake. I saw an apple fall, and there was a wild scramble and shrill outcry. Others came tumbling down, and we could hear the children dashing about all over.

The youngster in the tree was enjoying himself tremendously. He gave another leap astride his bough.

There was a little thud close beside me and, out of the corner of one eye, I saw a large rosy apple bounce from the grass above to land, as I felt, on the leaves and twigs covering the neighbourhood of Burk's head.

There was a slight movement from the body beside me and a rush of little feet. I saw a child about to jump down into the ditch on top of us, and instinctively I turned my face to the earthy wall and pressed my head down.

In that second I heard an angry voice. '*Was macht ihr, Kinder? Kommt her!*'

The jump was never taken, the merry voices ceased suddenly. I could hear the angry tones of a man bidding the apple-raiders come out of the spinney. The children were evidently very subdued. We heard their feet rustling away through the grass and climbing the wall. Then their footsteps died away; the voice of the man, still scolding, died away too, and the little wood was quiet.

I turned my face to the light again. It was growing dusk. I felt a movement beside me and saw Burk's hand and arm come up through the covering leaves. It groped about and presently it came down again holding its prize – a big fat apple.

For a few moments there was a sound as of some large rodent at work, then a hand gripped my arm, and I felt something pushed into my hand. It was the remaining half of the apple, all plastered about with wet leaves, but none the worse for that. I bolted it, leaves, core, and all in a few seconds, listening the while to a low and highly-coloured monologue from Gerrie regarding the manifold wickedness of children.

We eased our positions, venturing to free heads and shoulders. Night was falling, and the sounds of the farm activities were stilled, except for the rumble once or twice of a returning wagon at some distance.

We slept then and did not wake till the moon was high.

Chapter 17

Escape Day Five:
9–10 September (Sat/Sun)

I think I could have slept on for ever, but Burk woke me with a vigorous shake and told me it was high time we were on our way. I was unwilling to move. 'Man,' I said, 'how on earth did you wake up? I could sleep for years!'

'Damned owls!' he said laconically and, sure enough, I could hear a couple of these night birds calling to each other, one at some distance, and another somewhere in the treetops above us – and a weird and blood-curdling noise they made!

We decided to get away at once, only stopping to gather what remaining apples we could find and, of course, rousing the farm dogs by our movements.

Scrambling over the further wall we made for the nearest hedge, and, keeping behind it till we had crossed two fields, we got well out of sight of the farm before we sat down again and had a short meal. It consisted mostly of apples, for we had to be as sparing with our small remaining store of food as a sailor adrift at sea.

Then we took our maps and compass and studied them intently. We had made quite a different route from that drawn out before the start, but by now we were approaching that part of our original plan which lay within fifteen miles or so of the Dutch frontier. The little town of Epe, we reckoned, could not be very far away, and we must make for that.

It was the night of Saturday, 9 September. We had already been four nights and almost five days over our adventure, and the most dangerous part of our attempt was before us, the crossing of the frontier.

The bright moonlight made the risk doubly great, and the long strain was telling on us terribly.

When we rose, packed up our belongings, and trudged on again, we realised how much strength we had lost. The night became misty with ground fog, and there was no elasticity in our stride. Frequently, we stumbled over small unevennesses of the ground. Where before we had pushed shoulder first through the hedges, we now found it necessary to take more time. I cannot remember anything of that night's happenings, except the difficulty of progress and the frequent sensation that we were lost.

Sometimes we had to stop, and Burk would lie down flat for some minutes. His heart was over-strained, and he had several alarming attacks of pain. My own breathing seemed difficult and irregular after any extra effort, and I was troubled by a vague sense of impending failure.

I think we hardly spoke to one another; and now and again, I found myself in a semi-conscious state, stumbling along blindly, careless of direction.

I seem to remember struggling with barbed wire at times and that I reopened the gash on my finger made on the first night of our escape. My hand throbbed painfully, and there were ugly sores on my almost naked legs.

We cannot have travelled for more than two or three hours before we felt utterly spent. We had not set out till midnight, and by three o'clock we had begun to peer about for a place in which to spend the day. We chose a tiny copse in the middle of a large grassy field. The place was an ideal hiding place – just a few low trees, thick and bushy, with a mass of prickly undergrowth and high grasses. The place cannot have been more than fifteen or twenty feet across, and we crawled in and burrowed and wormed our way under the tangle of brambles and branches. We found a few early blackberries, not yet ripened, and chewed and sucked at these, for our meal of apples seemed very unsatisfying.

As daylight approached, we fell asleep among the thorns and briars and slept until we were slowly recalled to consciousness by that sensation of lurking danger to which we now seemed to respond instinctively. There seemed to be a pounding in my ears, and I wondered vaguely if it could be my own pulse. But the sensation of danger grew. I could see that Gerrie was listening too. The pounding noise had died away. It had stopped. Then it began again.

'Thud, thud, thud!' It sounded like the galloping of hoofs in the distance. We drew ourselves forward and craned our necks, but the noise was behind and we could not see through the thick undergrowth. 'Thud, thud, thud!' This time it was drawing very near; it grew louder and louder, and the ground seemed to quiver.

We stared in amazement. There was a huge bull in the field, evidently mad with rage. It passed quite close to us, round the copse, and we heard shouts and cries at some distance. I had a distressing feeling of sickness. The creature looked so monstrous as we lay on the ground. We could see its sides heaving and its tail lashing as it circled round our hiding place.

Then a group of men and boys came into view, carrying ropes and pitchforks, and there began a strange and exciting chase, which we watched with fascination. Sometimes the bull would dash off, with the men in pursuit, but more often it was the bull which did the pursuing, scattering his tormenters right and left in his rushes.

This was all right so long as they kept to the far end of the long field, but we dreaded every moment that the enraged brute would charge down our way and that one or other of his frightened hunters would dash for cover into our refuge.

I felt I would rather meet the men than the bull. For what seemed quite an hour, pandemonium raged in that field. The men and boys ran, shouted, and flourished their weapons; the bull bellowed and snorted and charged up and down. Two dogs barked and bounded, fortunately too excited over their work to bother about anything else; and we lay under our bushes alternately fascinated and alarmed by the turn of events.

Suddenly the bull, with nostrils quivering, stood still not fifty yards away. It seemed that he scented a concealed enemy. His tail began to lash from side to side. He bellowed with rage. I felt as a mouse must feel when a cat is about to spring, too paralysed to move, and not daring to shout.

Then I saw the great head with its ugly horns go down, there was a pounding in my ears, a sickening feeling in the pit off stomach and the bull was upon us!

He dashed straight into the tangled mass of trees, briars, and twisted undergrowth before us. We squirmed and wriggled, scratching ourselves heedlessly in our efforts to draw back as far as possible quickly enough to avoid the beast's struggle and remain hidden. Never have I heard such bellows of rage and fury! The earth and sods flew away from his pounding hoofs. He seemed to become entangled with his own efforts to free himself, and now his hunters were upon him.

We cowered down, not daring to look any more – only hoping in the excitement to escape the men's eyes, for the whole struggle was taking place not a dozen feet away. Fortunately the brambles and thorns were too thick for men on foot to push through. They must have thrown ropes round the animal from behind him. Rents and scratches were nothing to us, squeezed between prickly branches and moist earth, so long as we had avoided those terrible horns.

And when the bull was led away and we found ourselves still alive and at liberty, I was terribly sick. I felt ill and shivered all over. Burk lay so white and still that I feared his long over-strained heart had given way altogether.

After a time, when I felt sufficiently recovered, I dragged Burk's head and shoulders free of the briars and forced a little water from my bottle between his lips. To my great relief he opened his eyes, and a little colour ebbed back into his face.

Once Burk's heart was revived, however, his spirit – that spirit of revolt – could not be quelled, and he told me just what he thought of that bull. I had heard his views on children a few hours ago; before that he had expressed his opinions about German cows; but now he let himself go in a veritable epic of invective.

All that day we lay in our little copse. We could hear what we thought to be distant church bells and from study of our maps judged them to be the bells of either Nienborg or Metelen, north-east and north-west of our position. We discovered with a shock of unpleasant surprise that the hedge bordering the field on the north side ran beside a road – and a busy road at that – for we could hear the noise of motor traffic, and towards midday we made out a long line of horse soldiers and could distinctly hear the jingle of their accoutrements.

We had to allay our hunger with more raw blackberries, for we dared not eat what remained of our store – one army biscuit each and half a stick of chocolate. We smoked a little, finding comfort in so doing, for though it was Sunday, we did not anticipate any interruption from strollers as there was no path through the field, and it was not likely that any workers would be about farm business.

We did fear for a time that some excited boy might return to point out the scene of the bull's capture to an interested companion, but as time passed we grew too weary to care much what happened and, crawling well under our thick cover again, we slept.

Chapter 18

Escape Day Six:
10–11 September (Sun/Mon)

As usual, it was Gerrie who woke first. He said it must be after 10.00pm and time for us to start again. We had a wild hope that another night's march would take us right over the frontier if we set off at once, but we reckoned without considering the growing weakness of our bodies through exposure and lack of nourishment.

We did not like the prospect of crossing the road, which we now knew to be a highway, and probably guarded. We made our way to the hedge on our right and, sheltering under its shadow, we followed it to the angle where it met the road. At this point there was a gate, and crouching behind the gate-post, we watched the road for an opportunity to cross. Fortunately, there proved to be another gate on the opposite side of the road, and we hoped, should we chance to be observed from a distance, to be taken for farm dwellers on a legitimate journey home. The awful state of our garments would not bear close inspection, however, so we waited till a suitable moment should arrive. Two cars flashed past, but we saw no pedestrians, so we boldly opened the gate and hurried across into the opposite field before the headlights of another car appeared.

We thought we saw a light in the sky in the north-west, which might have betokened the town of Metelen, but the only houses we saw were those of farms and scattered cottages.

We crossed a railway line without any mishap and entered an area of larger fields, well watered by small streams, some of which we jumped and others we forded.

At one place, an orchard adjoining a small cottage, we helped ourselves to apples and stumbled on very wearily through a rather boggy district. We found it necessary to lie down frequently, and now and again we took a tiny sip of our crème de menthe and alcohol.

We were now approaching the town of Epe. It lay – a long line of houses, some of them whitewashed – shining in the moonlight right before us. We had meant to avoid the town and circle round it, but we appeared to be approaching it on its broader side, and the long straggling line of buildings extended as far as our view, north and south. We could see no lights, and though reason cautioned us to pass out to one side or other and so round an end of the town, our eagerness to reach the frontier and the fatigue such a detour would cause, decided us to push straight on.

We saw no lighted windows; the place was as quiet as the grave, and as we drew nearer, gave an impression of one long street. We had but to keep to the shadows, cross the street, dart in between the houses opposite, and we would be through the town, saving a two mile detour.

And this we did. We got through an orchard, but not without rousing its watchdog, and passed through a narrow alleyway between two house ends. Keeping in the shadow, we looked up and down the deserted street, and taking advantage of another dark patch, we darted across the road. Two more minutes in this eerie town of sleeping shadows and Epe lay behind us. We experienced a few moments of intense mental elation.

No more hesitation and bungling now; no more exasperating sense of being lost and not knowing in what part of the country we were.

We knew that between Epe and Enschede our route lay clear before us – west-north-west – a brief eight or nine miles, with no town or village if our map told us rightly. We could not hope to make Enschede that night now, for the nearer we got to the frontier, the more surely must we expect danger and move with caution; but given a decent hiding place through the next day, we felt that if our luck held we might hope to be in Holland the following night.

We found a general rise in the contour of the land once we were beyond Epe. The country became rough, and we met with patches of moorland and bogs. And here we had our first misgivings as to the speedy end of our journey.

We fell, and lay where we fell, frequently. The slight rise from one height to another tried heart and lungs to bursting point, and we floundered in bog land with scarcely the strength to lift one leg after another and to drag our feet free of the clinging morass.

We were now on open moorland and had struck a sort of bridle path rising up a rock-strewn incline, when a curious feeling of approaching danger brought me to a halt. I knew we must be within five or six miles of the frontier, but I cannot explain how it was that on this seemingly deserted moor I so suddenly felt the urge to take cover. I experienced a strong distrust of the track, and dragging Burk with me, I cut away to the left among the rocks and heath.

Five minutes later we distinctly heard the sound of several voices. We dropped flat, in a little hollow, behind a screen of turf and heath, and hardly had we done so than four military figures topped a slight rise to our right and came down the track we had just left.

The men whom we saw descending the moorland track were obviously military guards, either coming from duty or about to take up posts to our rear. We cowered low in our healthy hollow and watched them as they passed not thirty yards from us, their rifles in their hands, chatting and laughing light-heartedly.

We blessed the strange intuition which had urged us from the beaten track. Had we continued upon it for another five minutes, we should have been seen, and the presence of two figures on the moors breaking away at the sight of soldiers could have ended only in our capture or death.

While we realised how fraught with danger our advance must now be, the sight of the guards cheered us immensely, for we felt that their presence showed clearly that we were in the frontier zone.

After lying for some time, listening for noises, we rose and cautiously continued our way up the slight rise until we could see for some distance ahead. There were no other moving figures, but we were careful to keep well to the left of the track lest others should be passing along it. Our progress was very exhausting. The track evidently avoided the bogs and sudden hollows into which we stumbled and wandered as in a maze. Once I fell and struck my head so heavily that I had to lie where I was until the dizziness and weakness passed. Burk, too, was only moving like a machine kept in motion by a spring liable to run down at any moment. We felt as oarsmen feel at the end of a long course, when every nerve and sinew is paid out. Only the knowledge of our nearness to the goal kept us going, and that only for a time.

After being almost sucked under by a clinging bog, we expended what strength and energy that remained in dragging ourselves free, and we lay on the brink covered with slime and filth, unable to rise.

I do not know how long we lay before we realised that day was approaching, and unless this was to be the end – death from exhaustion upon the moors – we must find some shelter and make a final effort to get into a hiding place.

We crawled till we found a furze-grown hollow, like a shell-hole, and there we lay, after feebly cutting some tufts of dry heath and furze and piling them on top of us.

It was Monday, 11 September. We finished the last of our food and we slept. I remember waking at night and seeing that the moon was at the full, but I could make no effort to move.

Chapter 19

Escape Day Seven:
11–12 September (Mon/Tue)

I slept again, and when I woke it was daylight once more, and I realised that a whole night had passed, and we had not made any progress. Even Burk, on whom I had always relied, had slept too.

Some of my weakness and illness had passed. I was hungry, but there was nothing to eat. It was more than twenty-four hours since we had tasted food, and there was absolutely nothing edible in sight, so I took a drink of our alcohol and lay down again. Burk still slept; and there was no sense in waking him to the misery of hunger, for we could not venture forth in broad daylight while hope still remained of a safe frontier crossing.

I took out my map and studied it. We must surely be nearing Holland and the town of Enschede: yet from the glimpses I ventured to take of the country in daylight, I could not see so much as a solitary farm.

Ahead of us, however, there appeared to be a wood of poplars, and beyond that, I thought, the moorland probably gave place to arable land again.

I searched about in my pockets for my diary, and while doing so I found to my great joy a few ears of oats, which we had gathered some days before. Burk, I knew, must have some too, so I nibbled and chewed and seemed to obtain some alleviation of my hunger from these few grains.

Presently, Burk woke up and looked about him in a dazed manner. I explained that we had slept for a day and a night, that this was the morning of Tuesday, 12 September, whereupon he cursed volubly because I had not roused him before when I had wakened in the moonlight. It was no use saying that I was too done up and ill to care how long we lay and that I knew he had been the same: so I let him continue, till hunger stopped his loquacity and he got busy on his meal of oats – if meal it could be called.

Then we discussed our chances and the probability that we were nearer to the frontier than the appearance of the country betokened. We took stock of each other in full daylight, and the result was not very comforting. Gerrie was worn, ragged and dirty. His face was bearded and gaunt, and his own mother would not have recognised him.

I must have looked a more ferocious wild man than he, for in addition to six days growth of beard, my legs were almost naked and covered with cuts and sores. My trousers had been so torn on the barbed wire at Rennbahn that now they resembled very little more than a pair of ragged bathing pants. I still retained my Belgian forage cap on one extremity and a pair of French army boots on the other; and the sight of me thus clad was too much for Gerrie, who went off into a fit of weak hysterical laughter. To my dismay, this brought on a fit of violent coughing, which was succeeded by a heart attack, and I realised that my companion was more fit for a bed in hospital than another night's journey, which however short, must be full of dangers and difficulties.

I ventured a little way from our hollow, taking care to remain hidden by the heath till I found a little channel of clear water, and, filling our water-bottle, made my way back to my companion. He drank thirstily and, when he was a little easier, I doctored my cuts and sores with the small 'first aid' outfit we carried. My boots, which had been almost new when we left camp, had stood the journey well, but Burk's were in a very bad condition, and his feet were sore and festering.

Chapter 20

Escape Day Eight:
12–13 September (Tue/Wed)

I do not know how Gerrie felt when we set off that night. He must have been pretty bad, though he did not complain; and I felt very groggy myself, and fearfully hungry. How we cursed the moon! It lit up the moors almost as brightly as sunshine. There was no cover except that of low furze bushes and heather, and we were obliged to proceed for the most part on hands and knees, since we dared not risk the chance of being seen by some hidden watcher.

Moving in this way, we took hours to reach the poplar wood, which had seemed so near by daylight, and as we drew nearer, we wormed our way rather than crawled, since we did not know what danger might lurk in its dark recesses, or what lay concealed behind it. However, all being quiet, we climbed the surrounding fence and made our way in between the trees. They were tall and close together, and it was almost dark in the wood; so we rose to an upright position and advanced warily. Suddenly I saw something that made me grip Burk's arm and draw him behind a tree. It seemed to me that I could see a small red light glowing a little way within the wood. It looked exactly like the end of a lighted cigarette. We crouched down and I could feel that Burk's attitude was one expressive question mark, though he did not speak, and I could only dimly make out his face turned towards me.

I dared not utter a word; the smoker, if smoker it was, must be only a few yards away. Crouching there, I waited an age; but the light did not move, and it struck me as curious that the sounds of our approach had not disturbed the stranger so much as to make him move his hand.

Then I saw another light, exactly similar, a few feet to one side and slightly lower than the first. I did not know whether Gerrie saw this, but he pulled at my arm as though to indicate that we should go back, and this we began to do, as quietly and carefully as possible.

Those two motionless little lights glowing in the dark wood had quite unnerved me, and I felt like breaking into a run, with a desire to flee from my own terrors.

We made our way back to the fence, and cowering down, we listened. Hearing nothing of pursuit and speaking in a low whisper I said, 'Did you see them? The lights?'

'Yes!' answered Burk. 'What could they be?' 'They looked like cigarettes,' I replied.

'They couldn't be cigarettes; they were green,' returned my companion, 'and I smelt no trace of tobacco.'

I agreed that there was no smell, but I insisted that the lights were red, much to Burk's annoyance.

'You're colour blind, aren't you?' he said irritably, and so hit upon the very fact which had been the cause of my fright. What were in reality green lights had appeared to me to be red, but this did not explain their presence in the wood or detract much from our uneasiness.

Proceeding on hands and knees, we suddenly came right upon half a dozen of these mysterious lights, and then Gerrie gave a stifled shout. 'Why, they are glow-worms!' he exclaimed, and picking something up with one hand, he laid it on the palm of the other. I looked at it curiously, for it was my first acquaintance with this curious little phosphorescent creature, and Gerrie explained that he should have known what they were at once.

Much relieved, we now rose to our feet and pushed towards the heart of the wood with less caution – but had hardly continued for ten minutes before we were again down on our knees in a very sweat of anxiety.

There, between the trees, which at this spot were thinned out somewhat, we saw, quite plainly in the moonlight, a sentry box!

The opening faced in the other direction; had it been otherwise its occupant, if it were tenanted, could not have failed to see us. Our approach, however, over the soft carpet of moss was not sufficiently loud to disturb the sentry; but we never really knew whether there was a sentry there, for moving again with the utmost caution, we made away to the right, and halted, uncertain which way to turn or what to do. Were we actually on the frontier line, and did it extend through the heart of the wood? We did not know, and the night was passing and something must be done. So we moved, like shadows, from tree to tree, starting if one or the other trod on a stick or rustled the fallen leaves. It was like some horrible journey of a nightmare, and the dark wood seemed to our imagination full of lurking enemies, watching, and ready to spring.

We could not make a straight course, and we felt ill and beaten. At one spot we found a rude shelter of turf and bark, like a gamekeeper's hut, and we wasted a precious half hour in circumnavigating this, only to come straight upon another shelter of branches. This time we were facing the entrance and saw that it was empty, though it had evidently been occupied recently, for the seat of sacking spread in it was dry, and there were several ends of smoked cigarettes and pieces of paper scattered about.

When we eventually got out of that wood without having encountered a soul, we were more dead than alive. Burk had a foot that was causing him great pain at every stop, and we felt that we must have something to eat at all costs.

We were glad, therefore, to see a building that looked like a farm on the far side of the wood, and though it lay some distance from our route, we made towards it in the same slow fashion as that in which we had approached the wood, in the hopes of reaching fields with something in them of a nourishing nature.

So it was with thankfulness that on reaching a fence we discovered beyond it a field of turnips. We secured a couple, and finding on nearer inspection that the building we had seen was only a barn, we sat down outside it against the fence and peeled our turnips. The juicy pulp was refreshing, but we found it very hard to chew and more difficult to swallow.

We were ravenous, and yet the stuff seemed to choke us. There was a pile of potatoes against the barn, and we tried them for a change, without any better results: but our aching voids were eased for a time, and we sat wondering just where we were, till to our surprise we discovered that the east was beginning to show signs of the approach of day.

We did not seem to have covered more than four or five miles in all that long night, and there was absolutely nothing to denote where we were. Beyond the wood we had encountered a barbed-wire fence, which might mean the frontier line, but there still seemed nothing but deserted moorland, though in the dim twilight between moonlight and dawn it was impossible to see far.

We were dog tired, and I think we must have been light-headed, for as we sat there, I seemed to hear bells and dirges and queer sounds ringing in my ears: I shivered as with an ague. There was a ground mist, damp and clinging, and a chill west wind. I felt feverishly hot one moment and cold the next, and when Burk peeped inside the barn and said it was full of hay, I think he was glad enough when I suggested that we should burrow amongst it and remain there. We both hoped desperately that we were on Dutch soil, for we felt we could go no further without food or assistance.

The barn was simply a roof, upheld by rough timber supports and occasional crosspieces. There were two stacks in it, one to the west, being a high firm mass of barley; the other, to the east, a rather lower, looser erection of hay. Hay was scattered round, and for a time we were content to lie upon the soft masses strewn about: but Gerrie, ever cautious, pointed out the danger of this. 'We don't knew that we are in Holland yet, anyway,' he said, 'and if we're not and any one comes into this barn, we're done for. This hay has been touched recently. If we are going to stop here, we had better make sure that we are properly hidden. We don't want to lose the game at the last moment.'

I knew he was making sense and dragged myself wearily to my feet. We ate some more turnip and then set about mounting the barley stack, an easy enough proceeding had we been less tired and ill than we were, but incredibly difficult at the moment.

With the aid of a short ladder and one of the uprights, we hauled ourselves to the top, and Burk suggested tunnelling down slantwise into the barley and proceeded with difficulty to drag out tightly wedged sheaves. I did what I could to help him, but my hand was so painful and swollen from my torn and poisoned finger that I could only use one arm, and it was a slow business. Burk worked feverishly, for the light was growing; and we were busy at this when we were alarmed by the sound of rifle fire. It seemed to come from in front of us, to the west, and rippled along over a wide span, intermittently. We were worried by this and began to have real doubts as to our position. Were we still on the German side after all then? A fear that we might be entering a new fighting zone beset us. Just before leaving camp, there had been a rumour to the effect that Holland contemplated throwing in her lot with the Allies, on account of the interference of German submarines; and at the thought of meeting with German troops, our spirits sank to zero. Yet hope remained, and presently we completed a tunnel sufficiently wide for us to lower ourselves into, and about ten feet long, at an angle making it possible for us to lie rather than stand.

Having with great difficulty completed this hiding place, we pulled and pushed in an endeavour to widen the place and use up the displaced sheaves; and getting well in, we dragged the others down on top of us. We had thought that once inside the stack we should find difficulty in breathing and that we should be in danger of suffocation. To our surprise, we found that far from being a warm and cosy shelter, the barley, exposed as it was to the cold west wind, was most chilly and uncomfortable. I was on the outside and felt the cold intensely later on, but when we first got in, we were too glad to lie still and recover from our exhausting efforts to give much thought to the fact that the barn was unsheltered and upon the edge of the open moor.

We had lain there for perhaps a quarter of an hour and were beginning to realise our discomfort, when we both heard an ominous sound. It was the rumble and creak of an approaching wagon, and we could hear men's voices, though they came to us only as a murmur. We waited, straining our ears in an agony of suspense, to catch the words. Would they prove to be those of friends or foes?

The wagon rumbled into the barn and came to a standstill. There were the sounds of men's feet, of horses' harness, and a cheerful whistling. Someone spoke in a low voice, but the words were drowned by the whistler. We were too well buried to hear anything that was said quietly, and we dared not stir while any doubt remained of the men's nationality.

And then we heard a voice, raised and clear – '*Hier halten wir dann*' – and a stream of German. So Fortune was having one more sportive game with our tortured nerves! Was this to be the last? Were we to be discovered, too weak and famished to offer resistance?

Other voices joined in the conversation, but we had heard enough to tell us that we were still on German soil. I seemed to be drowning in waves of bitter disappointment, for in spite of the rifle fire, and in spite of all our caution, I had felt confident that we were across the frontier. It seemed incredible that we had crawled and trudged all night and covered nothing more than three or four miles at the most.

Work went on for some time somewhere in the barn, and then I heard the sound of the wagon moving again. It rumbled out once more and seemed to be accompanied by footsteps and by the whistle; and when these died away the place was quiet. But we could see nothing, and we did not know how many had left the barn, so we lay in silence, wondering when it would be safe to speak and if a whisper would penetrate through the corn.

I began to pick the barley ears and chew them and Burk did the same; and presently we heard the rumble of the returning wagon. So we were not to be left alone! Once again we heard sounds of activity.

They must either be building the hay stack up higher or carting it away. We could not tell which. Sometimes we felt a heavy body press against the barley stack, and every minute we expected operations to begin above us. The second time the wagon departed, it remained away for a lengthy period; and we whispered to one another in the corn stack. We had just decided that we had the barn to ourselves, when back it came again and this time there were children with it, and a dog with a yapping bark. That yapping was persistent torture. The little beast evidently scented us or heard our tiny movements, and he kicked up such a shindy that finally someone must have thrown him on top of the stack, for we could hear him scratching feverishly above us, giving little excited barks. I felt that if I could have got my fingers round his neck, I would have gladly expended my last energy in throttling him; and I thanked heaven for Gerrie's wise precautions, which had once more saved us from immediate discovery. The men evidently thought the dog was after rats, for they bothered themselves no further about him; but we were far from comfortable. Stiff and aching in every limb, unable to make anything but the smallest movement, we were miserably cold. The wind seemed to blow through the stack as through a network, and I was chilled to the bone. Every moment we expected a pitch fork to be thrust into one of us, and we were thoroughly alarmed when we discovered a child had got on to the stack and was shouting and dancing excitedly above us.

That danger passed, however, and the men seemed to settle down to a meal, for we heard the sound of a pail or can, and the footsteps ceased. The voices sounded muffled, and we could feel pressure against our hiding place. I pictured the workers, seated with their backs to our stack, munching their midday meal; and my own hunger seemed terrible. There they were, feeding away, only divided from us by two or three feet of corn, all unconscious that within the stack behind them, two desperate Britishers were concealed. I imagined how startled they would be if an arm were suddenly thrust out and a hand grabbed for their food. I stuffed some more barley into my mouth and chewed viciously; then I almost choked. A whisker from the barley-ear was at the back of my throat. I tried not to cough and the tears rushed to my eyes. It was intolerable. If anyone has ever got a barley whisker in their mouth they will understand my sufferings.

A cough or sneeze now would mean discovery and the end of all our chances. I pushed my finger in my mouth and poked about till I was nearly sick, but at last I managed to remove the wretched thing.

The dog, evidently sensing my movements, began his infernal yapping once more, and then we heard a yelp as if he had been silenced by a blow or kick.

Once again work was resumed and continued till the cart rattled away for a third time, and the barn became silent again.

We waited and waited. There was no sound of feet or voices returning. Hours passed, and still we lay in our cold and cramped position, till the faint light that had penetrated the top of the stack faded and we knew that it was night. We could hardly move, but when we had forced our unwilling limbs into action and pushed away the sheaves that covered us, we saw the moonlight and struggled out on to the top of the stack.

We looked down into the barn. I drew a long breath. The haystack had entirely disappeared! Where it had been, only a few scattered whisps of hay remained.

Gerrie looked at the bare space in the barn and back at our untouched stack. He cursed softly. I looked at him, and I loved the sound of it. I knew it was to his wisdom that I owed, to a large extent, my present liberty, and Gerrie's oath was like a prayer.

We waited till we knew it was after ten o'clock before we got down from our stack and searched about in the hopes of finding stray crusts of bread. But we found none and had to content ourselves once more with barley and turnips. It was while we were eating these that there came again the ominous sound of rifle fire along the west from the direction in which we now knew the frontier must lie. It was a depressing sound, but once again we had had a wonderful escape, not altogether due to the foresight of either of us, and we felt that Fate must have something better in store for us now than capture by the frontier guards.

Chapter 21

Escape Day Nine:
13–14 September (Wed/Thu)

Before we set off that night we sat in the barn and smoked a pipe of tobacco, leaning against the stack where a few short hours ago our enemies had leaned. We reflected upon the wonderful luck which had so far favoured us; and the thought was like a new reserve of strength arming us for the coming night, for our physical condition seemed quite unequal to the ordeal.

We expected to see the farm from whence the wagon had come, but we saw neither a farm nor any further sign of cultivated land when we struck out. I have said that the barn lay somewhat off our route, and we now resumed our way to the NNW and found to our consternation that what lay immediately ahead of us was a large tract of peat bog. We had experienced something of these treacherous bogs before and were not anxious to repeat the adventure. We had heard of men being sucked down into these horrible depths, and in our weak state, we feared a similar fate. Not wishing, however, to make a detour, the extent of which we could not gauge, we plunged on. The bog extended for about half a mile – a half-mile of the most desperate struggle that I ever remember.

Frequently, we had to fling ourselves forward before the ooze sucked us too far in. Repeatedly we had to help one another out, and our stout cudgels proved invaluable in this extremity. In order to find safe footing, we were obliged to wind in and out and spring from mound to mound of rush-grown sods. Sometimes, in the moonlight, which was fitful as the sky was cloudy, we missed our footing and sprawled in the slime, and only the fear of perishing in this awful morass kept us going.

Eventually we succeeded in reaching firm ground and came after midnight to pasture land once more.

We saw before us two converging hedges, and thinking that they would provide good cover, should anyone be about, we passed in between them on a sort of cart track. To one side, beyond the hedge, lay a deep bush-grown ravine and on the other a little copse. Showers of rain blew on the west wind and made it difficult, when the moon was hidden, to distinguish things very clearly.

It was after one such shower that the moon, sailing out from her veil of cloud, showed a large building right ahead of us with a high barbed-wire barrier beside it. From the top of this strange structure a flag flapped, and at this unexpected sight we came to an abrupt halt. Looking back upon that moment, it seems strange to me that we did not realise at once that in all probability this was indeed the frontier and the custom house building.

So accustomed had we grown to avoiding houses and taking cover at the least alarm that our instinct was to keep this building at a distance and make a circle round it before resuming our way.

While we stood irresolute, our course of action was suddenly decided for us in an alarming manner. From the other side of the ravine came a sharp fusillade of rifle fire, and immediately we darted for the shelter of the hedge and crawled as rapidly as we could away from the barricade. Bang! Bang! Bang! Another volley shattered the silence. We heard no sound of flying bullets, but we could not doubt that the shots were intended for us and that we had been observed as we stood in the moonlight. Again a cloud hid the moon, and taking advantage of the momentary darkness, we rose to our feet and made a dash in the direction of the little copse which we had seen on our right when we emerged on to the track.

From this concealment we crawled out further to the right, in order to avoid the formidable looking building, for we dared not return thither, since at any minute the soldiers who had fired across the ravine might cross it and open fire at a shorter range, were we to offer them a target. So crawling in the moonlight and running when it was overcast, we made our way more in a northerly direction with what speed such a mode of progress permitted: but the panic we had been thrown into, combined with the unwholesome diet of raw potatoes and turnips, made us both so ill that we made very slow headway.

Burk was in front and I following. The ditch bent round to the west again, when we saw something that made us both stop and flatten ourselves out, hardly daring to breathe. To our right at twenty yards distance stood a sentry box. And there beside it in the moonlight stood the sentry. He was flapping his arms round his body to warm them, and he had leaned his gun against the side of his box. We peeped at him through the blades of grass; he moved a few steps this way and

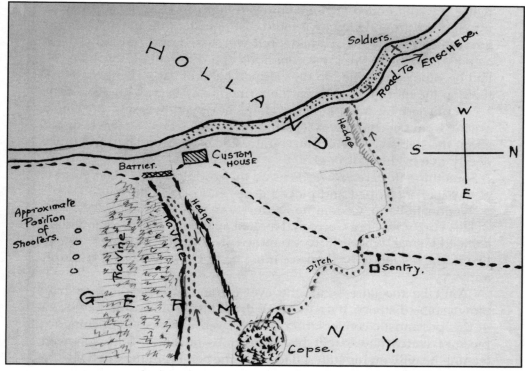

The author's diagram sketch of the frontier crossing made on 14 September 1916.

that, still flapping his arms, evidently quite oblivious of our presence. Burk moved slowly forward, dragging himself on his elbows; I followed, hoping frenziedly that we made no noticeable sound. Slowly and painfully, not daring to look again, we wormed our way on. I waited till the soles of Gerrie's boots moved a yard, and then I edged up into position behind them. In this fashion we advanced along that seemingly interminable ditch without any other cover for about an hour. We saw no other sentries and heard no sound of pursuit, and when the ditch made another bend in a south-westerly direction, we abandoned it, weary of this slow and exhausting mode of progress, and trudged on foot, taking advantage of the cover of a hedge. When at last we struck a road, which seemed to lead in the very direction we wished to take, we stepped on to it, with a feeling that if we were not now in Holland we never would be.

By this time the dawn was approaching. We sat by the roadside for a short time, conscious of nothing but our intolerable weariness. Then rising, we summoned our remaining strength and limped stiffly west-ward. In the growing light we could distinguish farms in the fields and a house or two by the roadside, but we passed and saw no signs of activity anywhere. We grew conscious of a different atmosphere. We had become accustomed to the German habit of early rising; half-past three in the morning had seen the farmer's day begun, his early tasks accomplished by lantern light. Here, however, we saw no smoke arising from the chimney-stacks and heard no clatter of harness or pail about the stable and byre. The countryside was still asleep, and it was nearly five in the morning!

Something fluttered towards us on the road. It looked like a piece of newspaper. I stooped and picked it up, and peered at it.

'Nationale Bank, Gedempte Oude, - - - - - - - Haarlem.'

This surely was not German. I looked again and silently handed the print to Gerrie, who in turn examined it. 'Dutch?' I queried. 'Seems like it,' he responded. 'Then we must be in Holland!' I said triumph-antly.

'Don't be too sure,' said the ever-cautious Gerrie. 'It may have blown some distance. It's a west wind, isn't it?' But I would have none of this pessimistic conversation and trudged ahead still clutching my piece of Dutch newspaper like a precious talisman. Burk followed, leaning heavily on his staff. I had left mine behind in the ditch, feeling that it impeded my progress and was of no further use, but now I would have been glad of its support, for I felt like sinking to the ground at every stop with hunger and fatigue.

We had continued in this way for perhaps a quarter of a mile, when we saw approaching us a little group of men. As they drew nearer, we noticed that they were in military uniform, and such a uniform as we had never seen in Germany, though it bore similar features.

Burk fell a little way behind, and assuming as casual an air as I could, I advanced to meet the strangers. They eyed me curiously, as well indeed they might, for Rip Van Winkle himself could not have presented a more fantastic figure; but they made no attempt to stop me, and with a gruff 'Morgen' I passed them. They answered with what sounded like a similar greeting, and I could feel that they had turned and were observing me with prolonged stares, but I continued for a few yards without turning. Then, anxious as to what had become of my friend, I halted and looked over my shoulder. Burk was in the midst of the soldiers, and as I watched in some anxiety, he beckoned to me. I retraced my steps, reassured somewhat by the lack of that ferocity which I had learned to associate with the German soldier. Burk too gave no sign of apprehension and appeared to be trying to make himself understood. I joined the little group and was favoured with another long but not unfriendly scrutiny. I felt that the suspense must be ended at once, and pointing at the nearest soldier I put the fateful question: *'Sind sie Deutsch oder Holländer?'*

Chapter 22

Freedom and Liberty

'Sind sie Deutsch oder Holländer?' We waited. How long did we wait? – God! Could they not answer?

Comprehension was followed by a look, half indignant, half amused. Then – *'Holländer!'* they shouted in chorus.

'Holländer! Holländer!' We were over! We were free! The blessed word rang in my ears; my heart sang with it.

I remember shaking hands all round. Everyone was talking at once – Gerrie and I babbling away in English and the guards in Dutch and neither party understanding a word of the other's language.

'Franzosen oder Engländer?' asked the Dutchmen in their turn. *'Engländer'* we replied, and there was more hand-shaking and a great deal of laughter and gesticulation in an effort to establish mutual understanding. We pointed to our open mouths and empty stomachs. *'Essen?'* we questioned eagerly. The men understood that. They rummaged in their knapsacks and produced chunks of white bread and polony sandwiches. Ah! The good white bread. We had seen none like it since our capture early in 1915. The guards watched with friendly smiles as we devoured their rations. We did not even bother to sit down. Forgotten were aching limbs and festering sores in this exaltation of relief and joy!

The men were all curiosity, but the barrier of language made it impossible to do more than convey by wide gestures and pantomime the nature of our journey and the distance we had covered.

'Enschede?' we questioned, pointing westward. They nodded reassuringly, and we made signs that we wished to be taken to the town at once; but they hesitated, evidently wondering what they ought to do with us and finally made signs that we should accompany them. This we did, somewhat disappointed to find that we were expected to retrace our steps in the direction from which we had come. But our fatigue was greatly mitigated by the good food and the overwhelming surge of happiness in the knowledge that our dangers were over and our purpose achieved; and if the way seemed long, we tackled it in good spirits. When, however, after going back as far as the spot at

which we had joined the road, and beyond, we saw the road curving to what looked like the very building with its flagstaff that we had seen by moonlight, we began to feel less comfortable. Was this some ruse? Were we to be handed over to the German authorities at the frontier? We did not know what arrangements there might be between German and Dutch frontier guards, but the friendly looks of our escort reassured us somewhat. The leader knocked at the door and a night-capped head appeared at an upstairs window. After some conversation in Dutch, the head withdrew. Another slight delay and we heard steps from within the building. A bolt was withdrawn and a further colloquy ensued. Finally we understood that we were to be allowed to go to Enschede under escort of one armed guard, and leaving the rest, who watched us go with a friendly smile, we set off for the third journey on that stretch of road. It was a long way to Enschede for foot-sore weary men, but the fact that we were on Dutch soil gave us heart for the journey.

The sun had risen and the little frontier town gleamed with the morning light on its roofs and spires. It seemed very quiet and peaceful as we tramped along its cobbled streets, to the great interest of a few early risers who stared at us curiously.

Our pilot led us to what was evidently the police station and there handed us over to an official and departed. We found ourselves in a room occupied by more guards, and we were evidently expected to answer a fire of questions put to us in Dutch. As we could make no reply in the same language, we were shown into a small empty room. The door clanged to behind us, a bolt shot home, and we realised that once more we were prisoners. Too tired to be much perturbed, we stretched ourselves at full length upon a long wooden bench, which ran across one side of the room, and promptly fell asleep.

We were awakened by the sound of the opening door and the entry of an officer. To our relief and pleasure he addressed us in fluent English and began by apologising profusely for his countrymen's discourtesy in treating us in such a summary manner.

He asked us our names and questioned us about our escape with evident interest and sympathy, punctuating our brief account with short exclamations of astonishment. 'But the frontier!' he exclaimed. 'How did you pass our guards?'

We protested that we had seen no Dutch guards, only a German sentry, and this statement seemed to astonish him more than anything else we could say.

We told him of the firing we had heard and of our fear of capture near the custom house.

'Yes, yes,' he said, 'but you must have passed our guards. They have orders to shoot anyone moving there between sunset and sunrise. There is a great deal of smuggling. Our men shot four smugglers only yesterday.' We shook our heads; we had not been stopped, we said, nor had we seen anyone but the German guard.

The officer seemed incredulous, but he was very polite. What could he do for us? We would like baths? Breakfast? We greeted these suggestions with delight and were soon enjoying the luxury of warm water and a clean shave.

The sight of our own faces in a mirror horrified and amused us, and we managed to make ourselves a little more presentable (as we had to dress in the same torn and muddy clothes) by pinning up the worst of the rents and tears, for, as Gerrie said, when I walked my legs went forward and what were once my trousers followed after. Our baths completed, we had breakfast: delicious hot coffee, rolls, polony, and cheese. After days of existence on turnips, bully beef, and army biscuits, this seemed a meal for the gods. Like gods we did justice to it. Meanwhile, the officer had been in telephonic communication with Münster, and what he heard from our erstwhile place of captivity evidently confirmed our story to his satisfaction. He was all congratulations and helpful suggestions. Our sores were bound up and my torn finger properly dressed: then, feeling like giants refreshed, we proposed a walk in the town and made our way towards the street door. At once the officer was all anxiety. We were tired, we must rest, he would make us quite comfortable. But we were anxious to taste our new-found liberty and assured him that we felt so refreshed that we were ready for anything. He protested against our desire to be gone and explained that the real reason for his anxiety was that our appearance would attract attention. In a frontier town like Enschede there were both Germans and pro-Germans, and he feared that our presence might give rise to some demonstration of the rival factions unavoidable in a community of varied sympathies. Seeing that he was obviously anxious, we agreed to remain where we were, and the officer, much relieved, asked what he could get for us. He sent out two of the guards for postcard views of the town [a few of these postcard views are shown in the plate section of this book], for cigarettes and chocolate; and on their return the soldiers eagerly acceded to the request that they should write their names and addresses in my diary. After a smoke we slept again, and shortly after noon, provided with a Dutch soldier for protection from German patriots, who might demonstrate their feelings violently, we marched to the railway station and caught the train for Rotterdam. On the journey we were objects of much interest to the other passengers. The presence of two ragged foreigners accompanied by an armed guard naturally roused curiosity everywhere, and when we changed trains, strangers plied the guard with questions and insisted on shaking hands with us. Others, whose sympathies were obviously German, eyed us askance, but for the most part we were surrounded by friendly faces.

I remember one Dutch boy, who could not have been more then fifteen, pulling out a case and offering us cigarettes, addressing us in French. When Burk replied in English, a delighted smile spread over the lad's face, and taking out another case from his pocket, he exclaimed eagerly: 'English? Ach then, have a cigar!'

At Rotterdam we were conducted to a sailors' home and there the guard left us. We were given cosy cubicles, and, after a meal, we turned in to enjoy the luxury of our first real bed for a very long time. Next morning we went to see the British Consul, resident nearby, and were received by him with smiling congratulations. He plied us with questions, which we answered briefly, and in reply to our request for a speedy passage to England, told us regretfully that we might have to wait some days as sailings between Holland and England had been much upset by the activities of the German U-boats. He promised, however, to let us know as soon as we could get a boat and enquired how we were fixed for money. As we had practically nothing, he supplied us with a pound and gave instructions to one of his staff that we should be taken to an outfitter and given decent clothes at once. We took leave of the friendly consul with many expressions of goodwill, his last words being a warning to avoid, in our sightseeing, any excursion to the mean streets near the docks at night, as the town was full of German agents, and cases had been known of French and English disappearing mysteriously.

A Dutch tailor next fitted us out with ready-made suits, being somewhat distressed that he could not provide me with one long enough in the sleeves and trousers, but this did not worry me much. I parted gladly with my own torn nether garments but made a parcel of the much be-pocketed waistcoat and the forage cap, and retained these.

That day, Friday, 15 September, our first real day of liberty, we spent wandering about Rotterdam. The presence of so much swiftly moving traffic confused us after so long an absence from civilisation, and I retain memories of broad streets through which the traffic hummed, edged here and there with grassy borders and miniature ponds.

We ordered tea for two at a smart café in one of the main streets. We felt awkward and shy before the display of spotless napery and shining silver, but we speedily forgot that in the enjoyment of the good food. When the waitress appeared with our bill, we scandalised the astonished girl by ordering tea for two again and by polishing it off with undiminished appetites.

On returning to our billet we were accosted by a cheery little individual who overwhelmed us with congratulatory speeches and urged us to accompany him to an English concert. We liked the friendly little man and followed him in the hopes of a merry evening. What was our consternation to find ourselves installed in the centre of a small gathering of very devout looking people, mostly females, and to realise that our cheerful friend had brought us to a mission meeting, in order, we supposed, to save us from the ensnaring charms of wine and women!

The 'concert' consisted mostly of hymns, and I am afraid my attention wandered shamefully, owing to the sotto voce interjections of my friend Burk, whose contributions could hardly be considered those of a religious nature.

We were further embarrassed by being introduced to the congregation as heroes, a name we did not feel we had at all deserved until we had stood the battery of the lady members of the gathering. While thoroughly appreciating the excellent intentions of this little community, we felt that the evening might have been spent more profitably, and I was glad to make our adieus and depart, for I felt that Gerrie's attempts at politeness would not stand the strain much longer. To relieve our pent-up feelings and moisten throats weary with well-doing, we adjourned to a little inn nearby.

As we sat over large glasses, quaffing the excellent lager-beer for which Holland is rightly noted, we found to our delight that the occupants of the adjacent tables were mostly English seamen of the merchant service. We listened enthralled to the conversations around us and heard for the first time the accounts at first hand of the dangers braved by these men in their everyday work. Hard-bitten, weather-worn captains and engineers these, who spoke of their escapes from drowning in a matter-of-fact way that testified more than anything to the continual risks and dangers they faced. Listening to their laconic sentences, we felt that we were mere babes in the art of evading or braving dangers, and that the greatest of our adventures lay before us in our voyage across the mine-strewn, submarine-infested waters of the North Sea. These men talked of ramming submarines as they might speak of directing coaling operations, and it was borne upon us how much the land we were longing to see owed to her mercantile service in those years of warfare.

On Saturday, 16 September, we took a short railway journey and visited the Hague and Scheveningen. We saw the famous 'Peace Palace' and saw also in another part of the city a number of interned British sailors, who had retreated from Antwerp into Dutch territory.

On our return to the seamen's home that afternoon, we found awaiting us an urgent summons to the consulate. We lost no time in obeying the order and found to our delight that the consul had news that a boat was departing almost immediately for a British port, and arrangements were made for our passage aboard. Our passport photographs had been taken before, on our first visit, and we had nothing to do but hurry down to the docks and embark.

I could hardly believe in my own good luck when we discovered that the boat was the SS *Grenadier*, a small tramp bound for Newcastle. We were shown our cabin and looked after with friendly interest by the mate, a grand fellow named Oscar Niederhausen.

Within half an hour of leaving the quayside, the *Grenadier* was rolling and pitching her way down the river in a manner that occasioned some doubts as to her seaworthiness once we were really on the open sea. The mate assured us that she could perform much finer gymnastic feats than those which were occasioning us some alarm now; a statement which did not tend to fill us with the enthusiasm he evidently expected, but we did our best to maintain a calm front in the face of his remark that we should meet with heavy weather beyond the bar.

We retired to our cabin after 10.00pm, feeling somewhat uneasy in the vicinity of the solar plexus. Gerrie took the higher bunk and I the one below, and we ostensibly settled to rest.

I had difficulty, however, in remaining in my bunk, and the large meal I had lately eaten had difficulty in remaining in *its* bunk. After a painful struggle of indecision, it evidently decided that it was not comfortable where it was, and I was obliged to get up and prostrate myself before a very small basin in a corner of the cabin. I was not cheered by the attentions of my cabin companion, whose unkind remarks were not calculated to lessen my sufferings in any way, and I felt a malicious satisfaction in the midst of my unburdening, when I was joined by a second victim of *mal-de-mer*. As usual Gerrie had some scathing remarks to pass regarding the cause of our present undignified position, but for once his voluble profanity was unable to maintain its customary flow.

At length we were able to return to our bunks and fall into a refreshing sleep, from which we awoke to find our boat awaiting the swift approach of a British destroyer, which communicated to us by signals. Niederhausen explained that the warship was giving us our course, that all shipping had to be minutely directed along channels between the mine fields with which the sea was strewn, and that the slightest deviation from that course might mean instant destruction.

The mate further informed us that the last four ships to leave Rotterdam had all been torpedoed by German submarines, and what with the fear that a U-boat might pop up out of the sea at any moment and the statement that the slightest mistake of the steersman might lead to our all being blown sky high, we began to feel that our adventure between Münster and Holland was a very poor little affair compared with this jaunt across the briney.

The prospect of being torpedoed, however, seemed almost preferable to the danger of being taken aboard a German submarine as recaptured prisoners of war. We concocted some sort of plan to meet such an eventuality, determining to pass as Americans, a plan which fortunately we did not need to put to the test, since it would undoubtedly have ended in failure. Most of the way northwards, from Orford Ness, we kept in sight of the coast, and we were amazed at the number of masts protruding from the water at frequent intervals, marking the last resting place of many a fine ship.

As the good old *Grenadier* rolled on up the East coast, my impatience grew, and I was loath to turn in for another night's sleep while those dear shores slid past. Early morning found me standing with Gerrie in the prow of the boat. The Durham coastline was taking form in the gathering light. We passed the mouth of the Wear and my eager eyes caught sight of Marsden Rock, standing out from the shore a little way beyond it.

And now we were off South Shields, and as we approached the end of the long pier, the throb of the engines seemed no louder than the throbbing of my own heart. To Gerrie, this was but another phase of his homeward journey, but to me the piers of Tynemouth and Shields were like welcoming arms stretched out to greet me. The old priory, the docks and wharfs we passed, the busy sounds and sights of Tyneside; these, these were Home itself.

I felt Gerrie's hand on my shoulder and knew he understood. We had ventured the road to Liberty together, and for me, this was the longed-for goal.

Epilogue

by Margaret Sybil Tustin

It was a warm afternoon in September, 1916. The classroom was stuffy with the odour that came from the sixty young bodies of twelve-year-old boys in the over-crowded desks. Every able-bodied male member of the boys' school's staff in this busy N.E. coastal town had been conscripted for military service. Women teachers had taken their place. I was fresh from college and finding the strain of such a class telling heavily on me. I had given the boys leave to read their library books, while I struggled with that bugbear to all teachers in those days of large classes: the attendance register.

But I could not concentrate on the endless figures. My mind wandered to someone else, more confined, more under strain than myself, to a young soldier in a German prisoner-of-war camp. He had gone out with his college company almost two years ago, and after a brief period of trench warfare in the desperate fighting of those early days, had been captured at Ypres with vast numbers of his comrades in the Durham Light Infantry.

We had met as teenage students, he in his second, I in my first year of college life in the old city of Durham, and fallen in love at first sight beside the wooded river, our sense of romance heightened by the fact that, strange as it must sound today, girl students were strictly forbidden to speak to, much less to go out with the men; and to do so was to risk expulsion.

But the outbreak of war had altered things somewhat, and Herbert and I had been allowed to meet, in the careful restrictions of the college grounds, in order to say good-bye to each other before his company was rushed overseas.

Now, a stranger in a strange town, I was living with my mother in lodgings. She was a widow: there were no pensions in those days, and now that she kept house for me, we were entirely dependent on my earnings. Somehow, we managed to exist on the £90 a year which was

Gefangenenlager 2, Münster i. W. (Germany).

Kriegsgefangenensendung.

Miss S. Simpson.

16 Prudhoe Terrace.

Tynemouth

England. N

Exact address of sender:

Name and christian name: H. Tustin

Camp; Gefangenenlager 2, Münster (Westphalia)

Block 4 .... Room 2. Working party

Dear Sybil.   30 · VI · 16 .

Your letters come regularly & cheer me
up tremendously. I like to think of
your having a jolly time. Make the
best of liberty. I never knew what it
was until I came here. I can't
grumble though for my own part — am in
the best room of perhaps the best
lager in Germany. And after all
— things always pass away.
I shall come back to you some
day — unchanged   Yours H

One of the many letters sent by the author from Rennbahn camp to Sybil, his sweetheart and future wife.

H. Tustin . Room 2 . Block 4 .

Gefangenen-Lager II
(Rennbahn)

Münster, July 26 · 1916
(Westfalen)

Dear Sybil .

    I have been thinking more than ever about you just lately, and I wish I could have a long talk with you . Letters are mere makeshifts, – and very poor ones at that .

    I often lie at night wrapped in the blanket you sent me, conscious of your photograph pinned beside your card of Marsden, on the wall above my head, my mind running back upon memories so sweet as to be almost sad, – and then I curse my luck, & myself, & the Scheme that grinds out our pittifully

---

A letter sent from Rennbahn by the author to Sybil, whom he was obviously missing. Written on 26 July 1916, when preparations for escape would have been quite advanced.

all my salary in those days. Life was pretty grim: there were Zeppelin raids over the coast, the war news seemed to grow worse from day to day, and the terrible casualty lists grew ever longer.

But for me the dreariness was brightened occasionally by cards, and more rarely by letters, brief and formal, from Herbert, and by frequent visits to his family only twenty miles away. I had refused, through shyness, to visit them before, but when a telegram had reached me in college telling, after weeks of terrible uncertainty, of his capture, I had made myself known to them and been received with open arms. Indeed, these visits were my only extravagance and recreation, apart from much looked-forward-to hours spent on the sea, fishing from a small rowing boat owned by a kindly fisherman, who welcomed my companionship.

How Bert would love the freedom of that little boat, the sea breeze, the sun on the waves, I thought, as my eyes strayed to the far patch of blue sky, which was all that could be seen through the classroom's one window, set high in the drab, brown-painted wall. Only that morning, I had climbed to the attic above the rooms we rented, to view the prospect and idly watched the approach to the river entrance of one of the brave merchant ships that had successfully navigated the mine-strewn sea lanes beyond. When would this dreadful war be over? When would Bert be free to come home again?

I bit my lower lip to keep it from trembling. Young Charlie Brown in the front row was regarding me with interest. Hastily, I bent again to the task of making the attendance numbers for the term check correctly.

At four o'clock I saw the boys out of the cloak-room, said good-bye to the rest of the staff, and went to catch my bus. To my astonishment my mother was waiting at the gate. Her face was white, she did not speak, but motioned me aside out of the crowd of outgoing boys.

What was the matter? She had never come to meet me before! 'Why ...?' But the question died on my lips as she thrust a telegram into my hands, her eyes intent on my face.

My heart stood still. A telegram in those days so often meant disaster. I read it and read it again, relief, bewilderment, and a wild joyful hope following each other in an upsurge of emotion.

'Come at once, H escaped. William.'

'Escaped' – Herbert! Escaped! Where to? I looked stupidly at the piece of paper, then at the place and time of handing in. It was from

Herbert's home town, evidently sent by Mr or Mrs Tustin, his parents. Where was he? How did they know?

My mind in a turmoil, I looked at my mother. She had never viewed with sympathy the fact that at eighteen I had met and fallen in love with a penniless student, the eldest of a large family, whose father was a village school-master. I was now her sole support. No wonder she viewed the prospect of losing her only child with fear and grief. But she knew that long months of separation had done nothing to turn my thoughts in any other direction, in spite of the fact that voluntary YMCA work had brought me in contact with many members of the Forces.

Now her own eyes were bright with excitement.

'You must catch the first train, dear,' she said. 'I've packed your night-things,' and she thrust a small case into my hands. 'The telegram came an hour ago. Let me know what it all means in the morning. You've just time to catch the 4.30.'

I dropped the bag and flung my arms round her. 'Oh Mother!' was all I could gasp, excitement and gratitude almost choking me.

Seated in the electric train, I read and re-read the brief cryptic message, seeking to extort more meaning from it.

If Herbert had escaped, he must be free somewhere. With his regiment again? In Holland? Or ... But I dare not let myself imagine anything beyond that.

I had to change from the coast-line train and wait for the little steam one. The short journey in that seemed endless, stopping as it did at small stations every two miles along the ten-mile run. There was no one to meet me when I alighted. They would not know when I would arrive, I realised, missing the boisterous twins, who usually met me on a Saturday, to drag me off to see some bird's nest or their latest acquired treasure. Four brothers and one sister – what a wonderful family they seemed to me, an 'only one'.

As I hurried through the long village street my mind raced ahead of me. What would I find or learn?

When I reached the house, I could see no one at the windows, nothing to tell me what to expect. I went up the garden path, knocked at the door, and waited. I thought I saw a window curtain twitch, heard voices in the passage, ... then silence.

It seemed ages before the door opened, and when it did, my knees almost gave way beneath me. Speechless, I gazed at the tall gaunt figure standing there in an ill-fitting civilian suit much too short in the sleeves, at the hollow cheeks and dark sunken eyes.

'Herbert!'

I don't know what feelings were reflected on my face, but he made no attempt to embrace me. He might almost have been a stranger as he took me by the hand and led me inside. Immediately then we were surrounded by his family, his twin brothers wild with excitement, the two older boys smiling proudly, his sixteen-year-old sister starry-eyed with delight, and behind them, his father and mother, gazing happily across at us both.

It was Herbert's mother who came forward and took me in her arms, saying over and over again, 'Isn't it wonderful, darling? Isn't it wonderful?'

Then we were all in the sitting room, everyone talking at once – 'When did you get the telegram?'

'What did you think when you saw it?'

'Bert, tell us all about it again, for Sybil to hear.'

'Tell us how you got over the wire out of the camp.'

'We couldn't say more on the telegram because it all has to be kept very secret.' At this point the door opened again and another oddly clad young man came in. 'This is Gerrie Burk,' said Herbert, 'who got away with me.'

I felt my hand seized in a hearty grip, and a Canadian voice drawled, 'I sure am glad to meet you, Sybil.'

I looked at the speaker. He, too, looked strained and worn, but he was not so alarmingly thin as Herbert.

At last I was able to gather what had happened, the outline at least of the story whose details were gradually filled in during the ensuing week.

Herbert and Gerrie had made their escape from the prisoner-of-war camp by hiding in the camp hospital, a building beyond the electric-wired barrier, but surrounded by an eight-foot barbed-wire fence lit by arc lamps and patrolled by a couple of sentries and a watch-dog on call. On pretext of visiting friends there with books, they had seized the opportunity to hide under two of the beds until a moment decided on previously. Then, as the sentries met and exchanged remarks at one side of the block, two patients had held up the dog. At the same moment, Bert and Gerrie made their dash, climbed the eight-foot wire and, tearing clothing and flesh, hurled themselves over, to roll down the sloping bank below. Then they had picked themselves up and run for it, knowing that since no alarm had been raised, they would not be missed until roll-call, an hour later.

Gerrie was something of a back-woodsman, and it was largely due to this fact that they had escaped detection during the ten days in which, often rain-sodden, they had lain huddled in ditches, covered by boughs skilfully cut by Gerrie from overhanging hedges.

Travelling by night, hiding by day, always hungry, their small initial stock of food only eked out by turnips or berries, they had had many miraculous escapes from recapture. Eventually, on the tenth morning of their adventure, they managed, without knowing it, to evade the frontier guards, and it was only a piece of newspaper, printed in Dutch, that indicated they were on friendly soil. Even then they dared not believe it, thinking that perhaps the wind had blown the paper over on to German territory.

It was only when, too exhausted to make a run for it, they met, in the early dawn, a party of soldiers who addressed them in Dutch, that they realised they were actually safe in Holland.

The kindly soldiers had pressed their packed lunch upon them and escorted them to the nearby town of Enschede, where they were housed in the police station pending enquiries. The results of these tallying with their story and no weapons being found on them, they were sent to the British Consul at Rotterdam, fitted out with what clothes could be found for them and, as free men, shipped on the first boat leaving for England and the River Tyne.

Even then, they were not safe, for previous boats had been torpedoed and their crews either drowned or captured.

My enquiry, 'When did you arrive home then?' brought a chorus of excited replies – 'This morning.'

'Just at dinner time.' 'Just today.'

'He just walked in!'

'We came into the Tyne at exactly eight o'clock this morning,' added Bert.

I remembered the cargo vessel I had watched from the attic that morning as it passed between the lighthouses of the two piers. The time has been exactly eight o'clock,

'I saw you. I saw the boat,' I said in wonder.

I shared a bed that night with Herbert's sister, Elaine; but it was hours before we fell asleep. My own heart, in spite of its rejoicing, held uncertainty and confusion. I failed to realise just what a terrible strain the last fortnight had been to the escaped prisoners, on top of months of privation, to make allowances for the utter exhaustion that lay behind the joy and relief of their successful bid for freedom. And on top of this it had been an evening of endless callers, for everyone in the place had heard the news. Even the village band had come along to stand in the roadway rendering 'He's a Jolly Good Fellow', followed by 'Tipperary', 'Keep the Home Fires Burning', and other war-time favourites, with a sincerity and gusto that made up for any lack of technique.

Bert and I had not had a moment to ourselves, beyond the brief time at the door on my arrival, and I felt an unreasoning doubt and hurt that our first meeting, after the long period of separation, had not been as I had always pictured it – a wild rush into each others arms. This was not the light-hearted boy I remembered, but a man, tried and tempered by all he had seen and suffered. I wondered if he really loved me. I did not even know whether it had been his own suggestion that I should be sent for, and I had not liked to ask.

The next morning Herbert and Gerrie had to go up to town for further questioning by the authorities. I went with them, and while they were interviewed, took the opportunity to dash home and see my mother, tell her the amazing story, and collect further clothes to take back with me, for Mrs Tustin's last words to me had been, 'You're coming back, my dear. Herbert will want you here all the time,' adding with an affectionate hug, 'We all want you. You know that.'

'Herbert will want you.' But did he? He had not said so, nor had he attempted to kiss me before Gerrie. He had taken it for granted, however, that I would be returning, and we met again by arrangement for the short journey in the steam train.

At his home reporters were waiting, but he had been forbidden to give any interviews, much to his own relief.

After lunch his mother glanced at him.

'There'll be more callers this afternoon, my dear. If you'd like a rest ...'

He sprang to his feet. 'Come on, Sybil,' he said. 'Let's get out of this, I feel like a walk.'

We went out at the back door to avoid curious eyes and took a little lane that led out of the village, past fields where, only a few weeks before, the twins had insisted on showing me the enormous craters made by bombs dropped harmlessly from raiding Zeppelins. Today war seemed far away, the countryside aglow in the September sunshine.

We were alone at last, but a constraint was still between us. Nervously I kept up a string of questions, to which Bert made answers that grew shorter and shorter till at last we were walking in silence. Presently I caught his glance, almost furtive it seemed to me, and I turned my head to hide the fact that my own eyes were full of tears.

We were well beyond the houses now, walking under a blazing canopy of beech boughs. Suddenly Bert stopped, turned, and with a totally unexpected movement swept me into his arms. Taken so unawares, I would have fallen, had he not held me to him in an embrace I could not have broken from if I had wished to. His lips found mine with a fierce hunger that frightened yet thrilled me.

'If you knew,' he said at last, 'If you knew how I have longed for this, lived for this! Tell me you still love me, Sybil.'

The autumn twilight was falling when we made our way home again. Our faces must have reflected the joy in our hearts as we joined the family circle for the evening meal, for never do I remember such a happy gathering.

'What have you done to him, Sybil?' his father asked, his eyes twinkling at me across the table. 'He looks worlds better already!' His mother gave me a look of gentle understanding.

And indeed some of the unhealthy pallor that had so shocked us on first seeing Herbert seemed to have gone, and I knew in my heart that it would not be long before he was completely recovered from his ordeal.

But there was a different ordeal before him, for the village had decided to honour their hero, and there was a celebration in the local hall. Herbert, considerably embarrassed, had to listen to accounts of his boyhood exploits, recounted by local worthies, and comply with requests to give them the story of his escape, which he did, as briefly as possible. He was then presented with what is known as an 'illuminated address' and a cheque for £25, while his family and I sat there trying not to look as proud as we felt.

For now, secure in the confidence of his love, I no longer felt a secret envy of others' claims to his friendship and acquaintance. I enjoyed to the full the praise and congratulations he received and was proud to accompany him everywhere. He went to see my mother, who had never even met him before, and she put aside doubts and anxieties that I was too inexperienced then to appreciate, and welcomed him warmly. In the early afternoon of a beautiful sunny day, we took my fisherman friend's boat, he proud to lend it when he learnt whom it

Friends in Ponteland and Neighbourhood
Desire to express to

Private A. Tustin

8th. Durham Light Infantry,

their appreciation of his courage and ability in successfully escaping from Rennbahn Prison Camp, near Münster Germany. His friends also wish to give him their congratulations and good wishes on his safe return to Ponteland on September 18th, 1916.

Signed on behalf of the Committee

Fredᵂᵐ Langton   Chairman.
Vicar of Ponteland.

This 'illuminated address' was presented to the author on his return home to Ponteland: 'He [Herbert Tustin] was then presented with what is known as an "illuminated address" and a cheque for £25, while his family and I [Sybil Simpson] sat there trying not to look as proud as we felt.'

was for, and we rowed out towards the lighthouse, past which Herbert had sailed so short a time before. And to think that only a week before, as I told him, I had pictured him in captivity and longed, hopelessly, to have him with me just where he was now!

The following week Herbert was to go to London for an interview at the War Office, but we had two more days to spend together. On the Saturday night, at his home, we sat before the fire in the old-fashioned kitchen, which seemed suddenly deserted, our feet on the polished steel fender.

Herbert drew something from his pocket. 'Darling!' he said, and something of his earlier hesitance and awkwardness seemed to return. 'You know I have no job to go to when the war is over, as yet. And I'll have to rejoin my unit, get a commission I hope, and see the thing through. I will probably be sent abroad on garrison duty; they don't send an escaped prisoner back into the firing line. I haven't a bean, as you know. It isn't much of a prospect for a girl like you. But if you love me enough to wait, Sybil, could you ... would you wear this?' And he took from its little case a ring of rubies and diamonds. 'It's not an awfully good one,' he went on, 'and I couldn't even have got this if it were not for that presentation ...'

Wordlessly, I gave him my left hand, and he slipped the ring onto the third finger and took me in his arms.

'Did you wonder,' he said presently, his eyes bright with teasing laughter, 'why they all left us alone in here?'

At the end of another half-hour, there was a hesitant knock on the door, followed, after a pause, by its opening. George and Norman, the twins, stood in the passage.

'We ... we just came to see if the fire was all right,' said George, very red of face. They took one swift look, but not at the fire, and rushed away, forgetting to close the door. We heard their excited stage-whisper.

'She's got it on! Sybil's going to marry our Herbert!'

Envoi

Many years have gone by since those days, years of joys and sorrows, of heavy family responsibilities, struggles, bereavements. For that is life. But through it all, years of steadfast love.

I am alone again now, as I have been for the past twenty years. Another war has come and gone. A son has followed his father's example of courage and daring in exploits of which Herbert never lived to hear. A daughter has given me three small grandsons.

Again I look out of a classroom window, on such a warm September afternoon as that one far back in 1916. As I watch the boys and girls I now teach, and see those I have taught growing up, falling in love, and marrying, under the incredible shadow of the H-bomb, I think of Anna's song in *The King and I*:

> 'Be brave, young lovers, wherever you are ...
> I had a love of my own ...'